# Positive Thinking

Quiet Your Inner Critic and Build a Strong Foundation for a Positive Mindset

*(The Most Efficient Guide on Positive Thinking, Overcoming Negativity and Finding Success & Happiness)*

**Larry Jackson**

Published By **Jordan Levy**

## Larry Jackson

All Rights Reserved

*Positive Thinking: Quiet Your Inner Critic and Build a Strong Foundation for a Positive Mindset (The Most Efficient Guide on Positive Thinking, Overcoming Negativity and Finding Success & Happiness)*

## ISBN 978-1-7774976-9-9

No part of this guidebook shall be reproduced in any form without permission in writing from the publisher except in the case of brief quotations embodied in critical articles or reviews.

Legal & Disclaimer

The information contained in this book is not designed to replace or take the place of any form of medicine or professional medical advice. The information in this book has been provided for educational & entertainment purposes only.

The information contained in this book has been compiled from sources deemed reliable, and it is accurate to the best of the Author's knowledge; however, the Author cannot guarantee its accuracy and validity and cannot be held liable for any errors or omissions. Changes are periodically made to this book. You must consult your doctor or get professional medical advice before using any of the suggested remedies, techniques, or information in this book.

Upon using the information contained in this book, you agree to hold harmless the Author from and against any damages, costs, and expenses, including any legal fees potentially resulting from the application of any of the information provided by this guide. This disclaimer applies to any damages or injury caused by the use and application, whether directly or indirectly, of any advice or information presented, whether for breach of contract, tort, negligence, personal injury, criminal intent, or under any other cause of action.

You agree to accept all risks of using the information presented inside this book. You need to consult a professional medical practitioner in order to ensure you are both able and healthy enough to participate in this program.

## Table Of Contents

Chapter 1: The Benefits of Positive Thinking ...... 1

Chapter 2: Assess Your Way of Thinking . 9

Chapter 3: Ways to Overcome Negative Thoughts ...... 15

Chapter 4: The Power of Optimism ...... 24

Chapter 5: Who Are You? ...... 32

Chapter 6: Strategies to be Happy ...... 41

Chapter 7: Take Away ...... 51

Chapter 8: Living The Life ...... 57

Chapter 9: What Positive Thinking Is ...... 74

Chapter 10: The Benefits of Positive Thinking ...... 80

Chapter 11: ife Planning with a Positive Outlook ...... 85

Chapter 12: Conduct a Self-Inventory .... 88

Chapter 13: Determine the Causes ...... 90

Chapter 14: Your Participation ...... 93

Chapter 15: Disconnect ...... 97

Chapter 16: Human Nature and Self-Understanding ...................................... 103

Chapter 17: Discover and Understand Your Own Emotional Needs .......................... 107

Chapter 18: Support Sources ............... 112

Chapter 19: The Golden Rule ............... 117

Chapter 20: Influence on Others .......... 120

Chapter 21: What Is a Positive Mind? .. 122

Chapter 22: Starting a Positive Cycle .... 130

Chapter 23: Keeping the Ball Rolling .... 135

Chapter 24: Jumping over Traps and Pitfalls .................................................. 140

Chapter 25: Creating Success via Visualization ......................................... 147

Chapter 26: What it Takes to Become a Positive Thinker ................................... 156

Chapter 27: 22 Tips on Positive Thinking .......................................................... 162

Chapter 28: Have Adequate Sleep ....... 176

# Chapter 1: The Benefits of Positive Thinking

Cliché as it can sound, that half of-crammed or half of of-empty glass of water says plenty approximately how we view instances. The manner we respond to those situations is affected one manner or the alternative thru using how we apprehend the end result. By genuinely changing the manner we've got a have a examine that glass and the way it might gain us, we're already gearing ourselves inside the direction of a greater successful and first rate attitude. People might also say and can negatively dismiss it as being honestly "all in the mind" and it is actual, but in a greater first-class connotation. The thoughts is a completely powerful tool that might both take you locations or land you caught in a rut. The way we've a take a look at things and how we take motion all starts offevolved from our head; it's miles a battlefield anyhow. Positive questioning is a state of mind in which you try to educate your self to apprehend any scenario as some component of an asset or a bonus in location of a loss. It is a gadget of acquiring a certain viewpoint wherein all conditions can be deemed as a first-rate hazard of success. It will be difficult to extend inside the starting, however as quickly because it becomes a dependancy, you may be reaping all the blessings as indexed down underneath.

What are the blessings of Positive Thinking?

Optimism or splendid questioning has an entire lot of advantages starting from physical, highbrow, and emotional. Here are some of them that you could gather:

It will boom your potential to deal with stress.

Compared to horrible thinkers, individuals who suppose definitely might be succesful to triumph over disappointments and frustrations higher. This is because of the reality their minds are already set into movement about the things that they are able to do and manage in preference to the topics that they have got left out and cannot exchange anymore. Optimistic humans couldn't save you on "what went incorrect" but might moreover continue to "what's subsequent".

60,000 is the numbers of thoughts that a normal character has in line with day. If you'll be predisposed to assume negatively all the time, those thoughts are going to make you depressed. Studies have established that inmates can enhance their bodily and intellectual properly-being through emphasizing best factors of the scenario.

Optimism strengthens your immunity.

It has been observed that our thoughts has direct effect and effect on our body. Researchers have studied that the area in our thoughts that is related to terrible feelings, has a weaker response of immunity to the flu vaccine.

Also, in every different have a look at, college college college students are injected a dose of dull mumps virus beneath the pores and skin of the forearm. These easy cocktails cause a cell immune response, resulting in a small bump on the injection internet net page. Researchers then can estimate the energy of the immune response through measuring the bump. When the scholars revel in checks, homework, duties within the semester, their optimism levels upward push and fall. The result of the observe is not surprising. When optimism is going up, so did the cell0mediated immune reaction. When optimism drops, the immune device weakens.

It is proper in your health.

Over the years, nice questioning has obtained some health advantages along side fewer inclinations for depression, decreased risk of fatality due to cardiovascular troubles, and an prolonged lifespan. That is why it is crucial to take care of your mind if you need to take genuine care of your health.

Do you recognize that your mind can actually help you stay longer? According to a today's document inside the Annals of Family Medicine, men who go through in thoughts themselves at lower threat for cardiovascular disorder are one-0.33 lower than people who recall themselves at not unusual threat.

Positive thinking boosts motivation.

An thoughts-set that leans closer to positivity may encourage a person to appearance a assignment through and take dangers. This will help to procure your dreams faster and could have more threat to be successful.

Studies additionally display that terrible self-communicate may also want to make you much less in all likelihood to achieve your desires. Imagine you need to shed kilos and all you're questioning is "I am already obese, so ingesting any other slice of pizza obtained't don't forget," then you will in no manner shed pounds, proper? On the alternative hand, if you say to your self "I can do it!" whilst you pass on ice-cream, it is able to keep your spirits up and your waist length down.

It opens up opportunities.

Because your thoughts is not caught inside the past errors, someone's optimism should view all situations, even failed desires, as opportunities for achievement. A super mind need to view fear as a project in preference to an obstruction. For example, even as you are placing out together along with your buddies in a bar, a lovable girl smiles at you. You can each assume she thinks that you are cute, or she thinks which you appearance silly. Thinking the preceding one will make you need to start a communication alongside aspect her and who is aware of...

It permits a more harmonious courting.

A amazing logician may need to peer beyond someone's flaws and imperfections. This does not suggest that you are a person who may be without problem fooled. It honestly way which you be aware of that character's terrible person but may also choose out to check their right factor. People gravitate extra towards someone whose man or woman is welcoming and not judgmental. Positive thinkers also are more likely to offer any other person a 2nd risk, for that reason growing a courting greater resilient to issues which could decrease the tendency for separation or ought to avoid breakups altogether.

Optimism will increase your tolerance to pain.

Although humans could possibly assume that poor thinkers is probably extra tolerant to ache due to the reality they may be more likely to count on it, excessive satisfactory thinkers have a propensity to bear and triumph over it higher. This is due to the truth they view pain as a "vital evil" and could use it to higher themselves instead of act and live wounded.

It elevates power.

A notable philosopher holds a number of energy because he perceives a good give up to any intention. It brings about a rush of adrenaline to pursue the project handy and enjoys the way of conducting it.

It encourages others to be inside the same body of thoughts.

Being brilliant is contagious. An optimist might be able to encourage the human beings round him to persevere and in the end benefit the same purpose more efficiently.

There are masses extra blessings that a person can gain from wondering and staying awesome. Now which you have an idea on how optimism can fantastically have an effect to your existence, it's time as a way to begin being aware of the flow of your thoughts and the way it leads to a positive end result. The subsequent bankruptcy have to teach you on how you can determine your manner of thinking and what you may do about it.

If you enjoy this e book thus far, click on on proper here to depart a evaluation for this ebook on Amazon!

## Chapter 2: Assess Your Way of Thinking

Have you concept approximately your mind? Does that question confuse you? Probably due to the fact you have not however considered analyzing your personal concept strategies and the way your thoughts takes you somewhere even as you are confronted with ordinary subjects. Maybe you have questioned why a sure scenario befell however have in no manner asked your self why and how you spoke back to that particular circumstance. A terrific thinker does not handiest remember enhancing the scenario however moreover deliberates on a way to correct the mind-set or the reaction toward it. This calls on the manner to examine and afterward, improve your manner of wondering. Assessing your manner of wondering is the first step inside the route of obtaining a great mind-set. When you start to be conscious at the way you reply to conditions, you will be better in adapting and overcoming troubles. And so knowing which you have the electricity to change the manner you receive as true with you studied, you'll get a revel in of safety interior your self and would depart you unfazed regardless of what you undergo. Take check of some tips that will help you out in evaluating your non-public thoughts.

Be accountable together with your thoughts-set.

If you're familiar with the story of the two wolves, it's miles precisely the way your thoughts-set want to be with reference to being effective. As indicated on this tale, whichever wolf gets stronger is the handiest that you pick out to feed. Whether evil, anger, resentment and ego, or suitable, peace love, desire and serenity, it would always come right down to your preference.

A lot of human beings might likely blame their screw ups on everything round them on the same time as in reality, they do now not understand that it's miles their choice right at the onset of putting in location a selected aim that in reality stimulated the quit end result. Most of the time, folks who think negatively would pre-empt an final effects this is terrible and may fill their minds with a whole lot of doubt. They may want to vacillate among pushing earlier and pulling once more and will get pressured why it did no longer exercise session. On the opportunity hand, in case you set your thoughts proper on the start as to having a a hit purpose, you'll be able to enchantment to exceptional elements that might make contributions to the fruition of your favored final consequences.

Whatever your idea is, it's far your reality. That is why you need to commonly take responsibility in your attitude in the direction of any hassle. No one else has that degree of control to your mind however your self. So if you need to take keep of your thoughts, first, discover ways to emerge as aware about it.

Keep a magazine or diary to reflect to your mind.

First, you need to lure your terrible mind and determine out what they'll be. When you phrase that notion floating by using manner of, you need to lure it, have a take a look at it and ask "what're you doing in my thoughts?" Some examples of the poor mind are "I am now not truely really worth of wealth" or "I don't want to get promoted and earn better wages". These mind can be so ingrained in your brains at the same time as you recollect that childhood to the thing which you expect they are virtually everyday. What you want to do is to take a look at those thoughts and ask your self how those mind are there? Where do they arrive from?

When assessing the way you discovered, it is important to have a significant proof of your mind and feelings. Keeping a magazine is a traditional manner of helping an individual for personal boom and character development. By journaling, you may be capable of peek into your private mind, gaining notion into your moods and behaviors. At first, you may enjoy a bit awkward particularly if writing isn't always your wonderful in shape however after some time, you will be amazed thru how an lousy lot you will be capable of observe yourself simply thru a unmarried get right of entry to. All you want to do is to take a couple of minutes on the give up of every day to install writing down a state of affairs and the manner you reacted to it. List or write down all your bad and high super mind all at a few degree within the day. By doing this generally, you may be able to be conscious a sample rising or stimuli that come what may additionally additionally trigger a horrible concept. By tracing your perception strategies at the surrender of each day, you can create motion plans on a manner to control it and how to reveal your awful manner of questioning right into a exquisite one.

When you begin journaling, you want to be sincere about the way you felt approximately a positive situation and how you answered to it. If you aren't a natural creator, virtually create a list and be a piece greater centered. You can pick out your pinnacle 5 most critical terrible thoughts as well as remarkable thoughts all at a few degree inside the day.

You moreover need to take some time to reflect on the mind that you have listed down. If you had time to mag each day, ensure to have your mirrored image and assessment at the least as quickly as on the cease of the week.

Now which you have observed the way to end up aware of your bad and splendid thoughts, it might be much less complex in order to combat the ones which you want to take away and positioned into effect the ones that you want to maintain. By understanding the manner you watched, you may be able to control your thoughts-set inside the direction of any situation. The next financial smash may additionally need to offer you strategies on how you may in the long run overcome your horrible thoughts and train you on how you may use it on your normal lifestyles.

## Chapter 3: Ways to Overcome Negative Thoughts

If you are a herbal pessimist, you may think you have have been given already hit rock bottom in terms of perceiving the worst about a scenario. Your mind may additionally have delivered you to the non-public, darkest and ugliest area even as faced an sudden trade on your life. One easy challenge which includes passing a the usage of exam would deliver you right right into a frenzy of hysteria because of the awful mind which you permit indoors your head. A lot of people should discover it difficult to dismiss this way of thinking because of the reality they had been so acquainted with reacting this way that it is nearly automated.

Negative mind may want to come bombarding your mind and might overflow on your normal lifestyles if you do now not rein it in. As what we've got were given determined inside the preceding financial ruin, you normally have the power to pick out out which type of thoughts you want to entertain. If you are the shape of person who has end up exhausted with thinking about unfounded undesirable consequences, then you can begin overcoming horrible mind to your everyday lifestyles. Here are a few tips that you can test each time you revel in like pessimism is slowly taking preserve of your mind:

Choose happiness

As with everything that we want to appear in our lives, whether it's miles a long-lasting relationship, or a big friendship, or a way to lose those more kilos, the important aspect to being successful in all of those is to be intentional. Believe it or not, selecting happiness is intentional as nicely. Abraham Lincoln as soon as stated "Most humans are approximately as glad as they make up their minds to be", and it is actual. You must in reality take the ones vital steps in selecting happiness. Mind you, doing this is not a as quickly as in an entire life occasion. Like even as you wake up within the morning and determine that nowadays is probably an excellent day, then forgetting all approximately it whilst you step out of the room to face a massive pile of mess inside the living room. Choosing happiness is whilst you make a decision to do it second through using second of each day. You will discover that within the approach, there might also nevertheless be persistent terrible thoughts that could creep again up but deciding on to be glad time and again is a manner to fight the ones.

One element that you can attention immediately to stay happy is to rely your advantages. A lot of horrible thinkers generally tend to overlook approximately what they already have. Try to hobby at the topics that you will be pleased about, which embody your circle of relatives who, on your mind, created that massive pile of mess, or the truth which you have woken up healthy and prepared to face the day. When you shift into this way of thinking, it might be tough to observe worrying conditions the equal way again. You will find out that during spite of the difficulties, there are nonetheless plenty of factors to be happy about.

Speak affirmation to your self daily. It is one hassle to don't forget which you are able to some issue, however you may enhance this perception in case you definitely listen it from your self. Try the "I am…" statements wherein you could pick out out from a listing of affirmations that you could say. Just make sure that you cautiously create an honest, honest and applicable listing that you may use.

Start your day for your terms. You can also furthermore have permit circulate of your control over that alarm clock, however that doesn't imply that you can lose manage of your complete day. Establish an energizing and big everyday inside the morning to set your entire day toward success.

Challenge your terrible thoughts

It is commonly essential to recognize what's real for your lifestyles. Sometimes, we get so stuck up with horrible thoughts that we overlook about that maximum of them are illogical and almost always…unfounded. You may suppose "this has passed off to me earlier than, and it did now not flow nicely." While it's far proper that the idea also can look acquainted, that does not propose that it might yield the equal stop end result. One issue to be privy to at the identical time as you lean in the direction of negativity is to don't forget a situation objectively. Say as an example; your mind have to tell you "you normally fail checks." Try to assess it or write it on a chunk of paper and project it. "Always? How changed into I capable of graduate if I continuously fail tests?" "How can I fail some thing that I in truth have spent the time to put together for?" These are a few examples of reality that you could mission the horrific concept with.

Replace terrible mind with fantastic mind

Recognizing and sorting out the accuracy of a terrible notion is your first step into gaining a bonus over it. Once you have were given had been given located to discover and project those terrible thoughts, it might be less hard so that you can flip the ones into extremely good. Keep in thoughts, although, that converting your thoughts should no longer recommend that it is some thing that you can skip blindly superb approximately. Being positive isn't expecting something to show out to your select with none grounds. If you in all likelihood did now not hassle to practice riding, you then definately can not assume to bypass the exam thru sheer properly fortune. Be first rate approximately a appropriate outcome if you are a hundred percentage tremendous that you have finished your utmost to build up the brilliant feasible prevent result. Hope for the high-quality if you have finished your pleasant.

You also can mission your thoughts through asking it questions. But make sure that you carefully convey together your questions in this kind of way that it'd require a first-rate answer. So in place of asking "why is it so difficult to pass this the use of test?" try "How did I ever get this opportunity to stress my very very very own automobile?" Make a aware try and direct the focus of your questions to notable mind.

Stop blaming your self

Face it; now not everything is set you. So if a task isn't always going your manner due to unexpected times which you cannot manage, do no longer blame your self. It isn't always your fault that a selected BMW cut you on the road. Nor is it your fault that the reason strain within the again of you is abusing his automobile's horn due to the fact you are each caught in visitors. Most probable, they are going through difficulties themselves this is why they may be acting that manner. When you customize, you may have the tendency to get paranoid and will probable truly promote your self short. When you generally assume that everyone is towards you and that the whole thing is conspiring to take you down, then you could in no way attain your complete functionality. Rationalize and start focusing greater in your abilities and your intention. This manner, you may be able to divert your interest from matters that couldn't advantage or have an effect on you however best on subjects which you have manage of.

No to filter out wondering

Negative thinkers are guilty of clear out wondering. This is even as you will be predisposed to recognition on the horrible difficulty of a situation or when you handiest pay attention the lousy facet of a declaration. When you do that, there will be no room for positive complaint in your thoughts. Pessimists would possibly never view criticisms as exquisite, but best something that could restrict them from progressing. This kind of thinking should annihilate all types of capability that might be advanced, might exhaust any ardour which you have, and might burn out all of the selection which you is probably clinging to. There is some reality in looking on the "brighter element" of life; you could no longer comprehend it but searching at each the tremendous and negative aspect of a state of affairs would probable provide you a deeper perception and can help you in reaching your goals better and quicker.

You are nicely aware now of the outcomes of permitting terrible mind to your thoughts and on your life. With this statistics, you will be succesful to expose your pessimism right proper into a excessive nice thoughts-set resultseasily. Continue analyzing to the subsequent bankruptcy to take a look at greater approximately optimism and how you can take steps into permitting extra excessive quality strength on your normal responsibilities.

## Chapter 4: The Power of Optimism

A lot of humans should attempt to water down or reduce the electricity of being fine, dismissing it as just a kingdom of mind that could no longer have a eternal hold in a person's life. It might also sound uncommon to a person who has been too privy to wondering negatively about a situation. But you may find out that optimism is a manner of lifestyles that could provide you with an side to any hassle. It is that figuring out detail amongst achievement and failure. Optimism must assist you obtain your desires and will assist you in going through all of the responsibilities irrespective of the quit result can be. Take a take a look at a number of the steps under that would inspire you to examine your lifestyles with more fervor and positivity.

Start getting stimulated

A lot of instances, we search for motivation from the human beings round us. Making them liable for some thing very last effects a mission may have. It is easy accountable human beings at the same time as our goals aren't met, however motivation need to in no way come from all people however us. It can be less difficult said than completed, specifically if you have the propensity to suppose negatively. So how do you do it?

The first step to start getting encouraged is to move. Physically, honestly go with the flow. Stretch, jog, perform a little pushups, whatever it's far that could get your blood pumping inside the morning. When you're bodily geared up, it would set up eagerness to your thoughts and can prepare you to undergo the relaxation of the day. Get proposal from one of a type humans, watch movement photographs from personalities who commenced small and made it thru life because of perseverance and religion.

Just just like the ones successful personalities, you moreover can also want to start small. A lot of instances we discover ourselves drowning within the center of all our dreams that we've set and cannot finish. It is higher to begin and entire one small venture in preference to address masses suddenly and now not quit a few element. You will discover that you may be inspired greater at the same time as you spot those small obligations being completed one by one.

One of the strategies to get inspired is to go public approximately a certain aim. Say as an example you need to decide to losing 5 kilos in a month, placed up it in your near pals' and own family's timeline to make them your obligation companions on your development. Knowing that your family are searching your every step and getting affirmations from them should simply get your feet glued on that treadmill.

Flashback your achievements

It can be strange to pay hobby that you need to take a look at your past to move beforehand, however it's far actual and effective. But make sure which you nice take be aware and keep all the incredible training that you have discovered out of your past. If there is one issue that you may do a throwback on, it'd be your former achievements. This might without a doubt offer you encouragement to address something disturbing conditions you may be coping with. You can also additionally find out the strategies which you have used in advance than to acquire a cause and apply it to your modern-day duties. Have a good sized communique with people who've been with you for a long time and ask them their notion on the manner you have been capable of get past a fine hassle earlier than. These people is probably able to provide you precise insights approximately your man or woman that you may not have located earlier than. When you are capable of deliver substance in your former successes, placing fee in your modern-day purpose is probably an entire lot less difficult.

Eliminate Distractions

Sometimes it's miles hard to interest on fixing a specific task whilst your mind is bombarded with diverse matters. Just as fast as you make a decision to attention on a mission that your mind betrays you and your mind fly away. This offers you a feel of defeat due to the fact your thoughts cannot seem to govern a majority of those mind floating spherical your head which then effects in pessimism.

Take fee of your thoughts by way of information your very own fashion in overcoming challenges. If you are someone who goals tune to pay interest, pass earlier and flip up the quantity. On the alternative hand, if the song is a distraction, then ensure which you work in an surroundings that is non violent and can free your thoughts from any outside noise. You also can attempt to double-test your ordinary and behavior. You recognize that having social media up on your browser whilst seeking to carry out a chunk artwork could first-rate tempt you to test your feed and certainly divert your hobby out of your goal. If that is the case, then make certain to log out of all of your social media packages even as you're walking.

In addition to this, technology has been the most vital distraction in accomplishing a tremendous goal. It has the energy to sidetrack you regardless of how first-rate your resolve is in engaging in a assignment. Remember to control era and now not the other manner round because while used effectively, the era must useful resource you in attaining your intention faster and with extra average performance.

Be competitive

One of the vital elements in accomplishing a excessive excellent cause is to have competition and a healthy one at that. Being aggressive in a superb way must push you to show abilties which you idea you probably did not have and could educate you to be more assertive. Competition sans hate and greed could lead you to become an achiever. And on the same time as you're continuously giving yourself bear in mind at the same time as tackling a project, it is probably less hard as a way to check demanding situations and troubles in a extremely good manner. Eventually, time will are available which you will even welcome demanding situations and look in advance to fixing one.

Don't be afraid to invite for help

One of the trends that an individual should possess is being able to installation take delivery of as real with with the human beings round them. Remember that it is good enough to be susceptible at instances in particular while anxiety devices in. When you have got have been given humans round you whom you get hold of as authentic with, it'd be easier so that you can ask for assist whilst poor mind maintain to succeed to your thoughts. Trying to be remarkable is a awesome element, but there are instances while terrible wondering ends in a certain kind of tension that might already require clinical hobby. If this occurs, take that step to reach out to a person who has professional revel in on the subject of suffering with the worst form of pessimism. When to procure the power of optimism, you can have the capability to take manage of your mind. Once you have got located hundreds of those guidelines and try and exercising it to your normal life, it'd be now not feasible a great manner to study a challenge and not enjoy consistent that you could triumph over it. Optimism is a terrific thing in finding happiness in this in any other case selfish international. Let's pass at once to the following financial disaster to have a examine extra techniques for conducting that happiness that you have constantly dreamed of.

## Chapter 5: Who Are You?

Now which you have an concept on what happiness is and what its kinds are, it is now time to apprehend your self better by way of taking the time to evaluate your self. Do you adore your self sufficient which you are able to be glad? Here are some of the self-help questions you can ask your self and the way a great way to compare your answers.

Are you satisfied within the interim?

Do you need the way your lifestyles is proper now? Are you glad collectively with your method, your circle of relatives and the u . S . Of your existence? If the answer is certain, then you definitely truly simply is probably happy at this very second. Asking yourself this question lets you examine if you are happy so that you can preserve doing the topics that make you satisfied and to comprehend the things that aren't making you satisfied if you determined out which you aren't glad. This manner you could maintain being happy or stop the subjects that make you unhappy.

What are the subjects that make you satisfied?

Once you've already located in case you are happy or now not, you ought to now discover what the topics that make you glad are. When you discover them out, you've got were given to check it with the belongings you are currently doing. If it appears you're doing them already, then you definitely definately are doing an incredible job. If you've located out that you are unhappy, and you appear like doing the topics that make you glad, you need to determine out within the event that they without a doubt make you happy and if no longer, you want to look for the subjects in order to make you glad.

Are you at peace?

Now that you understand the topics that might make you satisfied are, it is now time to ask yourself in case you are happy with the manner your lifestyles goes proper now. Do you observed you're headed in the proper path, and also you are not concerned approximately the subjects that might appear on day after today? If your answer is sure, then you definitely absolutely sincerely are at peace.

Are you suffering?

If you seem to not be at peace, you would likely want to assume two times. Are there things which might be preserving you far from being at peace? What are these gadgets that are making you go through? Figure them out so you can dissect them and find out a way to address them.

Are you organized to determine at the form of happiness you truely favored?

You are without a doubt aware about the manner you sincerely are for the time being and what you revel in and why it's far now time to determine about the form of happiness you could pursue. Do you believe you studied you could cope with some most important adjustments on your existence so long as you're assured that you will be satisfied? If superb, then you can hold to determine what form of happiness you need to pursue.

Now which you have evaluated your self, and you apprehend how america of your feelings are and the way you genuinely experience, it's miles now time to know a manner to pursue your selected very last outcomes. How do you pursue actual happiness and achieve it at the equal time as now not having an excessive amount of trouble? Here are some of the belongings you must don't forget if you actually need to be surely glad.

Acceptance & Living the Now Onwards

The first actual element you need to apprehend whilst you are pursuing your real happiness is which you have for you to get hold of the matters you've got completed and get preserve of your past. You need to truly consist of your past even though terrible subjects have befell then. Focus at the winning and don't forget that the vital component to be satisfied and gather real happiness is to recognize that you are inside the gift, and there are despite the fact that masses of things you may do for your existence so long as you take shipping of the things that come alongside the manner.

All guys have sin

This is the a part of pursuing which you want to in reality accept which you are human too and that there are instances you can commit errors, and those mistakes can be visible as sins to the rest of the human beings searching you. Realize that this is normal and that those gadgets are certain to take location. The temptation is always right there, and there may be instances that you could deliver in to that. The key's to ensure that there are greater instances that you are capable of do the proper element. You should do your great in maintaining temptation out of your door and out of your heart in truth as nicely.

Whatever executed is carried out

The topics that have already came about in your beyond can't be modified, and the effect it has on your gift will continuously be the same. You do now not have the competencies to change the subjects which might be already accomplished. What you do have is the potential to change the manner subjects are going via using no longer repeating the identical errors which you have already done and usually doing all of your best inside the whole lot you do. You can commonly try to stay a better existence by using manner of the usage of doing the things you need to do the maximum on the right time. It is all for your palms, and all you need to do is to play the proper playing playing cards.

Repent and discover ways to permit flow into and remedy oneself of any emotional burden or guilt

A first-rate element about reaching happiness is that it is a way. You do no longer proper away end up glad, at least right happiness is not that manner. And due to the reality it is a tool, you may do things bit by bit so you can preserve your sanity intact. Repent for the matters you probable did wrong and gather that you have triggered these items. Let bypass of the topics which may be bothering you and the subjects which can be hurting you. When you relieve your self of any emotional burden and guilt you have got, you'll be capable of live a higher life and a happier one at that. So allow yourself be relieved from emotional strain and take matters easy. Do no longer allow your life be tousled due to the things which have already befell. You ought to study even as to permit pass and at the equal time as to keep on.

The secret's doing more ideal every passing day.

In order to free your self from the things which might be hurting you or are bothering you, doing pinnacle matters may assist you. Once you look at the artwork of selflessness, matters can be a whole lot much less difficult to you. There are things that you could fine be capable of feel whilst you do top deeds. Let your coronary coronary heart say the matters it wishes to say. Once you acquire the thanks from the people you've helped and spot the grins on their faces, you may comprehend that helping different people and displaying kindness and generosity is some component so one can pay off honestly properly. You can be capable of sleep better at night time and function desires which might be a long way higher than you've continuously had.

Believing and working towards the Universal Laws

There are matters called: customary laws that govern Zen happiness. They are your guide to accomplishing the happiness that lasts for a long term, if now not all the time. The secret is to believe in those felony suggestions and workout them via attempting to find to incorporate them into your each day existence. Some of those legal pointers are the law of Karma, the regulation of giving, the law of appeal and lots more. The subsequent bankruptcy will provide you with extra records approximately those legal tips and speak them very well. For now, you truly need to get an idea of what they're. As you understand, karma is a pressure that gives you decrease again what you have got given to specific humans, the law of giving is then one which tells you to offer to different people that allows you to be happier.

Optimism and the regulation of enchantment

Optimism is truely a key In being happy. When you constantly look on the best facet of things, you're able to see the hidden splendor that others do no longer see because of the reality they do now not problem looking. You need to live an constructive life as it makes you a lot tons much less depressed and happier. It helps you to no longer assume negatively approximately other people so that you can get on the aspect of them better. On the opportunity hand, the regulation of attraction is like attracting the matters which you need through doing subjects that are associated with it. This may be in addition stated inside the latter chapters.

This bankruptcy has taught you some of the subjects you may do to be able to benefit the happiness which you desire plenty. It is as a great deal as you to decide out how you will observe those items as a manner to be happy. At the quit of the day, your happiness however lies on your palms because of the fact only you may pull the reason to be a happier person. The subsequent bankruptcy will assist you to apprehend what to do at the same time as you've grabbed the happiness you've typically longed for.

**Chapter 6: Strategies to be Happy**

Who wouldn't pick out out happiness? No one have to allow himself to be lonely when life is providing him an possibility to live his lifestyles the splendid manner that he can. We are born to certainly to live our lives and to stay it abundantly. Happiness is probably elusive for maximum human beings. You may be a person who has been through some of struggling and disappointments and were aware of anticipate pain and loneliness as inevitable as day and night. Because of this, we attempt to discover happiness in the incorrect places and the wrong human beings.

Why does it depend, besides? Is it not enough to have the precise process which could pay loads? Is it now not okay to settle with someone who possesses brilliant capabilities but does no longer make you happy? Is happiness overrated?

On the contrary, happiness contributes plenty to someone's success some component mission he or she is taking. According to analyze, medical doctors who are glad have a propensity to offer greater correct and green diagnoses and will offer sufferers a enjoy of desire. Schools which may be extra focused on the emotional and social nicely-being of college college students have a tendency to acquire extra academic attainment and improve university college students' conduct. Happier humans make a contribution greater to society simply and are much more likely to be willing to gain out and help each distinct. They are much more likely to do volunteer paintings, vote and create a healthful network.

Happiness subjects masses due to the fact it's far our final aim in existence. It is probably driven too frequently at the backseat but deep in our subconscious, it takes precedence over all of the cloth topics that we've got had been given. If you want to take that first step within the direction of happiness, take note of the subsequent strategies that might jumpstart your life:

Setting up your aim

The first step to locating real happiness is to recognize what you want and paintings to accumulate it. There isn't some thing higher than installing location smooth goals and visualizing the steps to acquire them. When you count on a few thing, much like the fruition of a particular dream, you could sense your blood pumped up and get you obsessed on all of the possibilities spherical you. Anticipation may want to moderate up a mild bulb in our thoughts on every occasion you bear in mind all the topics that you are searching for to gain. When you have a motive to appearance ahead to, you may get a enjoy of motive and this means that on your existence. Setting up a goal makes you accountable and accountable with the route that you would love your life to go. Just like a compass that would constantly remind you in which north is, a aim may want to maintain you grounded and sane amidst all the craziness inside the worldwide.

Be precise approximately what you want. It doesn't rely if it's that European tour or a fantastic weight reduction, it's far critical that you are particular at the identical time as you're developing your dreams. If you have got were given were given some thing unique and concrete that you could popularity on, it might be lots faster if you want to get again heading within the right route even as you feel your reputation declining. When what you really need, you'll be capable of rally all of your property in the back of this specific goal. This manner that you may employ all which you have that is associated with that intention the wonderful manner and will avoid dropping time on subjects that aren't as crucial or as associated with accomplishing it. A quite smooth instance might be sacrificing that 3rd Starbucks espresso of the day and instead hold the cash to your dream tour. Investing on wholesome food as opposed to junk and processed meals would likely in reality diploma up your weight reduction purpose.

Break down your desires into achievable chunks. Avoid being too grand whilst you reflect onconsideration on doing a high-quality challenge to obtain your goal. If you're making plans on sporting a duration 6 bikini this summer time, then perhaps you want to attention your interest first on losing 5 kilos a month. When you spoil down a aim, you can avoid getting too crushed and disheartened that you may now not be able to attain it. When you advantage those smaller dreams, you may moreover experience a enjoy of pleasure that might encourage you to press on and go the more mile. Maybe a hint more than 5 pounds subsequent month is an additional $10 for your dream vacation. Also, on the equal time as you are making a mistake, it would be easier to smooth up and redo.

Vision Board and Inspirational Tool

Did you already know that our thoughts would possibly reply higher to visible stimuli? For example, you understand due to the reality you have already found from university what purple looks as if. You are very a wonderful deal conscious that the crimson shade devices off an extreme emotion be it love, anger or hate. But why is it that we feel angry or panicky when we gather an e-mail with a topic line this is in the red font? Seeing some component visually invokes an emotion that a easy idea of it may in no way do. The identical principle can be finished on your goals. It is one problem to take into account all the terrific desires and aspirations for your head, and any other to definitely see it written down. So how do you create a vision board?

Take time to visualize and write down your desires. It may additionally need to encourage you to take more assured steps into carrying out them. It moreover locations you within the right frame of thoughts at the identical time as you get distracted with the aid of subjects around you.

Relax and have amusing. A vision board which is likewise referred to as a life university should be an pastime that would positioned your mind and your spirit inside the identical and correct mind-set. Do not placed too much strain on your self specially while you aren't a herbal artist. You aren't looking to magically make the ones pictures seem for your lifestyles right now, discover your float and make this hobby a laugh for your self.

Go creatively crazy. When you have got got a particular motive written down, once more it up with pics, charges, inspirational texts and visible affirmations. Go all out with the images, some aspect that inspires you to reach your goal ought to be pinned to your board. Let the pride that you feel approximately accomplishing your desires gasoline your creativity but ensure that you are developing one cohesive board. Once done, bypass earlier and cling this in a conspicuous region on your room or your table. This manner, it would continually remind you of your cause at the identical time as lifestyles receives within the manner.

Changing your attitude

Changing your notion has masses to do with pursuing your dreams and reaching happiness. During the way of attaining for your dreams, you will find out that there can be masses of roadblocks and frustrations that would pull you down. It takes a person with a nice angle to certainly pull through and gather any intention. Changing one's mindset might not happen overnight, however being intentional and developing a conscious effort to have a examine the intense factor of a situation may also help you get for your goal faster.

Try to fight fear. This is the most important enemy of actual happiness. When you succumb to worry, you may promote yourself quick and might be given mediocrity. It need to make you develop tunnel imaginative and prescient, very last yourself off from better opportunities around you.

Love your self

This can be the most easy problem to do to accumulate happiness however loving yourself is something that might be hard to advantage. At times, it's miles less complicated for us to simply accept some different individual's weaknesses and flaws as long as they do now not issue to our very very own. We lavishly deliver gives to one in every of a kind people, spend time with them and positioned their goals first earlier than our non-public. Although this in itself isn't simply lousy, while you lose yourself in the system of creating exceptional humans happy, you then definately need to re-evaluate your priorities. It isn't feasible to provide a few element which you do now not have an abundance of.

So keep in thoughts that you additionally want to be loved and pampered.

Be privy to your reactions and emotions closer to positive situations. Do now not neglect approximately about or dismiss your herbal responses and try and be aware of your intestine. When you are self-conscious, you'll gain more perception and know-how of the manner you are as someone and might be more powerful in imparting outward love.

Do not misconstrue self-love as self-worship. Loving your self is accepting that you have flaws and weaknesses, on the identical time you excel on high quality trends and attributes. Self-love does not imply which you are above absolutely everyone else, on the alternative, it way that you fail at instances and accepting that it's far ok. It way giving your self a hundred% respect.

Visit a non violent region

All people crave that one glad vicinity whenever negativity surrounds us. It is critical then that you have a gap wherein you can unwind and in which you could have a look at a particular scenario looking returned. It does no longer have to be a far flung destination, a quiet spot on the rooftop, a park near your vicinity, anywhere wherein you can have a downtime and refresh your thoughts. This is a first-rate manner to begin turning your terrible thoughts into splendid. When your thoughts is loose from all the litter for your life, it'll purpose a better and extra first rate mind-set.

When you bought happiness, you'll locate that terrible mind haven't any energy over you. Living a greater excessive exceptional lifestyles may be much less tough and further gratifying now that you have triumph over negativity.

## Chapter 7: Take Away

Knowing the strategies of happiness and a manner to be excellent do now not surrender with mere information. Embracing the regular motions of living a effective life takes an entire lot of staying strength and consistency for it to work. It does not rely when you have dedicated errors inside the past or when you have failed miserably in accomplishing happiness once or twice. What is extra important is that you pass on from at the prevailing time ahead. Do no longer expect a knight and shining armor on his white horse who will rescue you and sweep you off of your toes, or a few different individual who will create your non-public happiness or benefit your private desires. Strive to be the hero of your private existence tale.

Give your self some time to change

As with any addiction, it takes time for someone to acquire definitely. The equal aspect is going with living a effective existence. With willpower, exercising and consistency, you will be able to master the potential of questioning quality. This does now not take area in a single day; you will find out that you may undergo pretty some usaand downs, and it's far k. It is how you will be capable of develop as a person.

Be healthful

It is not feasible to have a exquisite thoughts in case you do not feel physically well. Try to modify your terrible bodily conduct into nicely ones first, this way your thoughts can be satisfied that you are certainly prepared to live a first-rate lifestyles. Just with the aid of way of repute up instantly and working in the direction of correct posture could provide you with a enjoy of self perception that could get you assembly any horrific mind head on.

Smile often. You will discover that truely via smiling, you are sending alerts for your thoughts that you feel fantastic approximately your common well-being. Aside from that, human beings round you may gain from your smile; it can be the one detail so that it will enliven their in any other case horrible day.

Practice mindfulness

Be at one on the side of your feelings, mind and sensations. By schooling mindfulness, you can have a deeper notion and interest of who you're and what is currently going on round you. When you have got mastered this, you'll be able to harness more manage of your lifestyles and ultimately your personal happiness.

Meditating for just a few mins every day could take your thoughts far from the worldly buzz. This should help you advantage extra attitude on issues which you are having a tough time addressing. You also can be able to deliver your thoughts a few relaxation that would result in a sense of happiness.

Be revolutionary

You might not assume you are willing to be modern, however even you could have a nice problem of your self that yearns to create, to be innovative or to paintings collectively along with your fingers. Exploring your modern issue may additionally provide you with a enjoy of freedom. It could make you realize that there's every other manner of doing things that might be uncommon, however may want to but yield top notch results. Knowing which you are not stuck within the conventional way of questioning ought to get you to feel greater in fact towards a hard hassle.

Not anybody has a herbal propensity to be revolutionary. But that have to not save you you from taking schooling to take a look at a first-rate paintings that you have never completed in advance than. Taking up painting, poetry, pottery or woodwork might be a exceptional manner to start.

Go online and find out tutorials approximately nearly everything. If you experience the need to knit, sew or crochet then, there are hundreds of net websites and motion snap shots that provide useful facts on a way to begin.

Draw or sketch some thing comes for your thoughts. Write poetry or a brief tale. Take a loyal bounce and start a completely unique. You'll in no way comprehend what form of skills you have got been hiding all along except you attempt them out. Exploring your progressive facet presents a cathartic revel in that lets in your mind to reboot and be extra powerful in handling conditions.

Surround yourself with amazing humans

It is proper that positivity is contagious. Negativity is the identical manner. As with the story of the two wolves mentioned on this ebook, you've got the selection to feed whichever behavior you need to build up. You moreover have the energy to pick out out the sort of humans you want to surround your self with. When you often hold out with first rate folks that could provide encouragement and affirmations, you will be placing your self up for fulfillment anything direction you decide on.

But of course, in reality, there are folks who are close to us who might also have a terrible outlook on life. If this is the case, you then definately have the responsibility to tug them decrease decrease returned up and offer encouragement to transport on a adventure with you to positivity. Since you currently have the expertise on a way to stay an excessive quality lifestyles and in the mean time are reaping its advantages, it is high-quality trustworthy to skip it at once in your family who may need it the most.

Set possible desires in your life

Remember that regardless how small your steps are; they may though get you one step in the direction of your goals. Continue to work on attaining your desires. You will locate that you may be able to gain self notion when you start checking your listing, and you will have greater effective energy in lifestyles.

## Chapter 8: Living The Life

Now which you have already got an concept about how you'll pursue the happiness that you want from the previous bankruptcy, it is now time to study a extremely-modern lesson on the manner to maintain the happiness that you may be capable of have. You need to forestall taking matters as a right and make certain that you will be able to treasure the topics that you have and the love that has been given to you. Here are a number of the topics you can do to forestall taking subjects as a proper.

Be content material fabric with what you have

Every man or woman has their own percent of advantages that comes from the better being, but in case you are at the bottom of the meals chain, it's miles simplest natural to ask for greater, for a better lifestyles, for a higher tomorrow. The trouble is that maximum humans aren't contented with what they have and try to pursue happiness and achievement despite the fact that they must step on one-of-a-kind human beings. It isn't proper to disregard different humans genuinely due to the fact you have got got have been given a cause you have to acquire, and they're now not part of it. You need to like the things you've got had been given and be contented with them.

## Pay it in advance

Learn a manner to share the advantages you've obtained to others however the fact that it is a small one. For example, in case you seem like blessed with authentic meals and an abundance of them, then provide food to folks that want them. You want to understand that the blessings you received are alleged to be shared with different people and no longer just preserve for your very very personal sake. You should pay the stuff you acquired ahead to the those who may need them. Donate to charity; spend some time along with your family and friends to steer them to happy.

## Appreciate the little topics

People find out it irresistible at the same time as you are taking have a look at of the little subjects they do for you. They are touchy creatures that love being praised and being preferred. While most human beings do no longer have the manners to understand the things exceptional human beings do for them, you want to maintain for your mind that the humans round you are all preventing a conflict on their very private so that you can't blame them for the topics they in no way really lifeless.

What you do onto others will come another time to you

Have you ever heard of the quote from the bible that broadcasts, 'Do not do to others what you do now not need others to do to you.' So be beneficiant and offer people the topics you could offer for them and but set a restrict in doing so. Help those in want so that at the same time as you're the simplest in want, they may assist you as well. What it simply needs to mention is that you want to believe in Karma and recognize that what is going around comes spherical. See the best inside the entirety and absolutely all people

It is regular for humans to normally will be inclined to reputation at the terrible in preference to the best. Our minds commonly typically tend to hang to the poor with out giving a top notch deal attention to the excellent. It is so clean for human beings to discover the horrible. Thus, seeing the best in the terrible is a ability. Veer a ways from the norm. Go teach yourself to prevent focusing at the horrible. Don't look for weaknesses, but look for regions of development. Don't search for threats, but search for demanding situations. Don't examine failures, but see the motivation to attempt all over again and do higher. See the component? There is commonly some factor correct inside the entirety. Be grateful for all of the "lousy" subjects in your existence because they are blessings masked as adversities/catastrophe that you are presupposed to unmask and notice and experience the lovely modifications they bring into your lifestyles.

This goes to humans as well. See the best in anyone no matter how tough it's far due to the fact you have no concept what they have been through, or what they may be going via that made them the way they will be now. Drop the judgment, and apprehend wherein the other person is coming from. There are reasons why people are the way they may be.

Seeing the high-quality in the good deal and everyone won't be clean, but the happiness you'll get out of it's far properly worth it, not to say that it takes maturity on the way to take a look at this lovely capacity. If each people recognize a manner to look the good in the good deal and all and sundry, remember how higher off this international can be.

Stop worrying about what others may additionally anticipate

You have handiest one existence to stay, so don't spend it demanding about what others might probable suppose. Immature humans will criticize you besides, so truely do the topics that make you glad. Never ever permit humans's notion of you be masses greater critical than your happiness. The first-class man or woman who's allowed to decide you is your self. Why fear approximately what others may also additionally anticipate? You don't want them to love you besides. Bc so focused on dwelling your lifestyles that you haven't any time to consider whether or not or not or no longer others assume you are doing it right. If you rely your happiness on people's judgment of you, I guarantee you, you may stay miserably for the relaxation of your lifestyles. The experience of gratitude comes the on the spot you prevent stressful.

Take dangers

Go available and divulge your self to the arena irrespective of how horrifying it may seem. Taking risks is part of lifestyles. Do a few factor you've got were given never finished earlier than. Do some aspect that honestly scares you. Staying on your consolation zone offers you comfort, however going from your consolation place offers you a enjoy of success and accomplishment with a purpose to reason happiness. You don't get say thank you to disregarded opportunities, you in reality remorse them. Save yourself from the regret and say thanks for the revel in.

Make mistakes

There is not whatever wrong with being wrong. What is inaccurate is continuously being proper. Imagine your life with out the mistakes you have got made, do you located you'll be the man or woman you are now? Do you found you'll be wherein you're now? The wrong selections you've been beating yourself for are people who really lead you to the proper place. Don't be so scared to dedicate errors. If you don't devote errors, how will you be pleased about the property you idea you've got executed proper? How will you be pleased about what you have now? Mistakes will make you recognize that there's generally something to be pleased approximately.

Be the slight to humans's darkness

People find which means and reason. This is natural. You have one and simplest motive in this lifestyles, and this is to be a blessing to people. Make your lifestyles beneficial for others. Even if you are going through the darkest days, despite the fact that there may be an excessive amount of in your plate, despite the fact that the arena offers you all the reasons to hate your lifestyles, usually pick out to be the strong one and discover methods on a manner to help others notwithstanding your non-public troubles. Be the candle that could slight humans's darkness. By being a blessing to others, you may see how blessed you're in existence. Being a rock for others even if you yourself sense like falling aside is a diploma of real energy, and that power is sincerely a few component to be thrilled approximately.

Always supply yourself some by myself time

Being surrounded via people is healthy specially if the ones humans are oldsters which can be very outstanding, recommended and satisfied in life, however make it a factor to offer your self a few silence. Give yourself some time to meditate. Your me time are the instances you may prevent, sit down returned, loosen up and be aware how some distance who've come now, and be aware how stunning your life is no matter all of the annoying situations you are handling. At the forestall of a hard day, supply yourself the time to regroup even for as a minimum 10 mins. Your by myself time is it slow to vicinity your self together. Your on my own time is the time you get to realize who you're and what you are now. After spending time with your self, you'll find out your self grateful for in that you're, what you're, and what you've got now.

Life acquired't provide you with rainbows and butterflies, you want to create them, and going through the typhoon is part of the method. It's smooth to be happy about the good stuff, but it's miles the "terrible" topics we need to virtually be happy about because of the fact they carry out the nice in you, they create about out the strength you never notion you've got got were given. If you maintain a experience of gratitude irrespective of all adversities, you'll locate your self truly glad and contented in conjunction with your life.

To be able to forgive others and your self

You can't declare to have forgiven someone at the same time as you still keep grudges. Your potential to forgive is a actual energy which you need to be very thrilled with.

Forgiveness includes statistics in which the opposite man or woman is coming from. When you forgive, you're selecting to be the better individual. Forgiveness is likewise a sign of maturity. Moreover, forgiving others technique forgiving your self. Forgive human beings due to the fact you deserve that peace for your coronary heart. Forgive your self for forgiving others. Sometimes, forgiveness takes time, and that is k. You don't forgive in a direct, and that is regular. Don't pressure yourself because of the truth to be able to make forgiving plenty greater tough. Give yourself some time. For others, it might take a truly long time to forgive, but what's crucial is the willingness to forgive. Just forgive others no matter the truth that it is a superb deal a good deal less hard no longer to.

To shed bags

When you hold a grudge against someone, there may be that feeling of heaviness on your coronary coronary heart. The heavy coronary coronary coronary heart will stop you from being satisfied. Stop carrying that heavy bags. You simply want to permit it bypass. Release the bitterness. You'll certainly make your life hard in case you keep on carrying the luggage. Be strong enough to go away all the baggage at the back of and flow into in advance. I assure you, you'll be amazed at how glad you're after letting skip of all the luggage to your life.

To avoid burning bridges

It is so clean to burn bridges while you're certainly mad at a person. Sometimes, burning bridges is the primary hassle you'll recall at the identical time as you hate the individual at that second. Do now not allow this to seem. Do now not permit your emotions consume you up and motive you to burn bridges. If you believe you studied burning bridges will make you sense proper, suppose again.It might possibly make you experience pinnacle speedy on the identical time as all the emotions are there. In the long term, you'll regret burning bridges. Don't permit some factor temporary motive you to reduce some thing or a person out forever. If you're mad, definitely get mad, but don't burn bridges. You'll in no way apprehend while you'll need to bypass that bridge yet again.

To keep away from making your international smaller

When you're at war with a person or at the same time as matters aren't so nicely amongst you and someone or a few humans, it seems like you are residing in a miles smaller international. At some thing in your lifestyles, you've got felt this manner, right? Did you experience accurate about it? Exactly. The answer isn't any. Nobody receives to experience right on the identical time as she or he makes his or her global smaller. Those who expect it is good sufficient to make their worlds smaller are missing so much out on life. Those who experience appropriate about making their worlds smaller are simply faking it. Believe me, the sector is already small, so why make it smaller? There can be a time while you'll meet the equal person you hate another time. There can be a time while you'll see your ex all once more. See, in this lifestyles, subjects arise again and again, and it's a small global anyhow. Do no longer permit some aspect or someone have that lots power over you that you may lodge to growing your worldwide smaller.

To avoid disappointments

Most of the time, you will be inclined to keep a grudge towards someone at the identical time as that someone approach masses to you. That is because you felt betrayed due to the truth that individual or that some component mattered to you. After the whole thing you've finished for the individual, disappointment is what you'll get. It sucks, doesn't it? Now, avoid getting disillusioned via not preserving a grudge. See, if you are preserving a grudge closer to someone, and that a person has wronged you, otherwise you felt wronged through way of using the man or woman yet again, you'll feel disillusioned once more over that character until the whole thing that she or he does appears to disappoint you. It is as if each little trouble the man or woman does disappoints you. It will now be a cycle of disappointments despite the fact that there is not some issue to be dissatisfied approximately. Save your self from the disappointment. Do not keep grudges.

To truly detach your self from the damage

Holding a grudge over a person is planting the damage he or she has accomplished to you.It's appropriate enough to sense the ache, take pride in it in case you want, however sooner or later, detach yourself from that ache. If you maintain on shielding a grudge, you'll keep on remembering the pain. Detach yourself from the harm to loose yourself from the ache, however don't forget the lesson pain has taught you. Just detach your self from the ache, the sensation, now not from the individual. Detaching yourself from the pain isn't like detaching your self from the individual that has caused the pain. Most of the time, people get this incorrect due to the truth they detach themselves from the character, no longer from the ache causing them to be sour regardless of lowering ties with the character. Don't reduce ties with the individual, reduce ties with the pain itself. Forget approximately the pain, not the character.

Holding grudges received't make you satisfied. It makes you the loser due to the fact you're the most effective who's sour and unforgiving. Holding a grudge will make you feel horrible not quality for exceptional people however yourself as well. Do your self a large choose, prevent retaining grudges.

Remove the negativity for your existence

The first aspect to do to reduce that luggage you're sporting is to reduce it absolutely. Remove it; erase it or a few factor you want to do with it as lengthy as it disappears. Negativity is awful because it is contagious, it passes from one character to some other, and it can have an effect in your mind-set as properly as it spreads in the direction of your frame. Here are a few strategies you can do away with the negativity in your life.

Throw your horrible thoughts away

Most people regularly do now not understand that it is herbal for them to hold in thoughts awful mind. What you have to do is be aware about those mind so you can throw them from your thoughts and deliver some space for the extremely good thoughts to are available in. Sometimes, these horrible thoughts overpower us, and we provide in without a combat. Examples of this are pride and envy. The excellent factor to do is be privy to it, and in fact actually prevent considering them. It won't be smooth inside the starting, however even as you offer it your pleasant, you will triumph over it.

Ask your self what you need

This is an important way to get rid of your negativity. Ask yourself whether or now not you need to be happy or no longer. If you need to be happy, you could start by means of doing things in order to make you satisfied as mentioned within the chapters earlier than. In the case that you do now not want it, try to think extra in fact. Once you have were given taken the time, you could ask your self again till you offer you with a solution in an effort to satisfy you.

Look for folks which might be effective

One of the fantastic techniques to put off the negativity is to surround oneself with powerful topics. Friends who are tremendous have an impact on their friends to be superb as well bypass find this form of humans. Be around high-quality people and it'll surely rub off on you, the longer you hang around them.

## Chapter 9: What Positive Thinking Is

Everyone in the world wants to achieve success and to come to be as satisfied as possible. This can't be denied irrespective of how an awful lot misfortune has disrupted that herbal choice for happiness. Happiness is the handiest stop of living, and excellent wondering is the nice technique to accomplishing it.

Psychology researcher Remez Sasson defines incredible wondering as a intellectual and emotional dependancy or thoughts-set of leaning at the extremely good facet of things. It sees all subjects, mainly adversities, as disappearing and the whole thing turning out well in the long run. It is similar to optimism, it genuinely is a notion that the destiny promises best suitable matters.

A great logician downplays awful conditions and perceptions. They journey at the primacy of goodness and happiness and the whole lot that represents them. They believe that nature will assist man conquer all barriers. They are strongly satisfied that lifestyles is largely ideal and could yield first-rate what is good and replace what is horrible.

Positive Thinkers vs. Negative Thinkers

Sasson similarly states in her article, "The Power of Positive Thinking and Attitude," that a faulty response to misfortune and wrong breeding result in horrible wondering. Because of individual versions, people react in any other case to enjoy. Negative thinkers in a circle of relatives additionally impact one-of-a-kind members to turn out to be like them. That makes breeding and the company we pick very essential to fulfillment and happiness. Constant exposure to thoughts-set is a ways more infectious than bodily sickness. Keep in mind what Jim Rohn, an professional in personal mentality, famously exclaims in some unspecified time in the future of his seminars: "You emerge as the not unusual of the pinnacle five people you accomplice your self with". In exceptional terms, if you are continuously round awful thinkers, this will bread negativity.

There are many horrible thinkers round us. They are folks that get without issues discouraged, mistrust others, are uncooperative, and blow out of percentage the awful issue of a situation. They additionally discredit optimists and high excellent thinkers whom they describe as unrealistic and mere dreamers. Living is drudgery or ache they should go through. Nobody desires to come close to terrible thinkers.

There is Good News

Nonetheless, there may be a developing fashion—increasingly more human beings take shipping of as proper with that the arena is out to do us suitable. They see the moderate at the stop of the tunnel in spite of the mounting difficulties of in recent times. They recall that we're created for appropriate and that same proper will in the long run triumph over evil.

Positivism, great wondering, or optimism is brief gaining extra supporters. They agree with that immoderate first-class questioning is an effective method to all wonderful ends. The fashion can be seen within the fast profits of books and attendance at lectures and guides on excessive satisfactory questioning.

Positive wondering can be resorted to as a manner of surviving the onslaught of successive cutting-edge-day trials—faculty screw ups, own family quarrels and separations, lack of jobs, infection, and so on. The desire to maintain dwelling or drift on necessitates a change in outlook from lousy to awesome. Otherwise, it may be the quit give up end result of a personal enlightenment on the primacy of genuine over evil, as Sasson elucidates.

A Habit, a Way of Life

A fantastic truth seeker is not an strangely lucky man or woman who's spared from hardships or rejection, writes Sasson. Neither is he a dreamer or a person who has misplaced touch with fact. Rather, he's one whose ordinary perception of the arena and life stands on the conviction that the universe is out to do us accurate as opposed to evil or ache.

The super philosopher might also revel in misery or face screw ups like different human beings do, however he can go through them because of the reality he believes that existence or nature is built on goodness. Despite the prevalence of injustice, the seeming dominance of hostility, brokenness, and inhumanity itself, his conviction stays that accurate will triumph in the end. This is due to the reality he believes in a Supreme Ruler who controls all topics. This Supreme Ruler will solve all issues and convey happiness to this international within the right time.

The effective truth seeker is an optimist, interchangeably. His placing in advance or hopeful outlook is not quick-term. It does now not practice high-quality to select conditions, nor is it undertaking to moods. It pervades his entire being. It manifests itself in his normal further to superb activities and dealings.

Positive questioning is a personal way of life. Although the high quality thinker is as human as every body else, his perception in the supremacy of goodness pervades his whole person. He has americaand downs likes every body else but his optimism or superb outlook serves as each a shield and a manual or restore mechanism. It lifts him unexpectedly on the same time as he's taking place to undergo a fall. He does now not stay in a make-receive as real with international where no longer a few factor wrong ever happens, however his regular outlook on love and on life restores his equilibrium every time it malfunctions.

Because it is a subculture in itself, it is incorporated within him. His organization belief and want inside the victory and superiority of goodness feature as a springboard of his options. Almost nothing can overwhelm him or deliver him down. He has a healthy notion of ache and satisfaction. The adage, choice springs everlasting, is the electricity that drives his existence.

# Chapter 10: The Benefits of Positive Thinking

Physical Benefits

In her article, "The Power of Positive Thinking and Attitude", Remez Sasson

describes the effect, results, and benefits of this point of view in every thing of

human life. Because the powerful logician dwells in a generally high-quality and maintaining environment interior, he enjoys a immoderate diploma of strength and enthusiasm. He is a high-quality deal in the route of authentic health than a terrible philosopher or pessimist is. A healthy mind in a wholesome body is every other clever pronouncing that applies to him.

He loves to eat right meals however with temperance. His extraordinary outlook prevents him from going to physical extremes. He balances hobby with rest. He is privy to his limits and does now not overdo anything. He loves the outdoor as he loves quiet indoor engagements, like analyzing and contemplation.

The first-rate logician can get injured or unwell, too, however he heals quicker than a terrible philosopher does. As posted inside the August 2015 issue of the Canadian Medical Association Journal, the findings of sixteen research that had been achieved over a 30-365 days period confirmed that patients tormented by a huge fashion of scientific situations had been more likely to get over their ailments in the event that they predicted that they could do nicely in some unspecified time within the future of their healing. In assessment, patients who harbored doubts approximately their recuperation did not enjoy healing that end up as speedy.

A high-quality logician is cooperative alongside together with his medical doctor. As a surrender give up result, he enjoys better fitness and additional sturdiness. Moreover, he seems greater more youthful and livelier than a horrific philosopher.

Another adage, mind over don't forget, applies to the incredible thinker. Science has big proof to resource the effect of the thoughts over bodily fitness. The high-quality philosopher is greater proof in opposition to harm and disorder than a terrible truth seeker is.

A excellent thinker is aware of and follows the recommendations of fitness on nutrients, workout, adequate sleep, and right hygiene. A poor truth seeker, in assessment, ignores or violates the ones suggestions.

Social Benefits

His openness and pleasantness entice humans to him. He loves to satisfy more and more humans. He is involved in plenty of worthwhile advocacies inside the community. He attends events and community gatherings (and church/worship services, if he belongs to any spiritual organization). He is a delight to recognise.

As a outcome, he makes plenty of buddies. If he's a scholar, his outlook allows him to observe higher. At artwork, he accomplishes extra because of his openness. His superiors further to fellow humans suggest him for his outstanding mind-set closer to art work. This inevitably consequences in fulfillment.

Emotional and Psychological Benefits

The excessive great reality seeker is capable of coping with stresses correctly. His private attitude prevents hundreds of them from affecting him on the outset. When a actual crisis takes place, he appears for an answer in preference to wallow in misery. And at the same time as the situation cannot be solved, he accepts the situation in a mature manner with out regret or resorting guilty.

The top notch philosopher is a contagious person. He transmits his optimism to others, especially folks who are open to it. In a hard scenario, a pleasing philosopher is the solution. He appears beyond the damage or downfall and will increase the morale of those involved. He believes that maximum issues can be solved.

Mental and Intellectual Benefits

Learning is less complex If the mind-set is exceptional or improving. The mind of the wonderful logician is exactly attuned to obtaining new expertise. He is also excited to new interpretations or additions of what he has already decided. The poor truth seeker, in assessment, is disinclined or disinterested to exchange his view.

With all the ones blessings, it becomes smooth that turning into a terrific logician is lots greater worthwhile route of movement. But how exactly does one flow about it? The succeeding chapters will communicate in detail the 10 easy steps to attaining lasting success and happiness because of extraordinary questioning.

## Chapter 11: ife Planning with a Positive Outlook

Before we get started out, it'd be prudent to first attention on in that you need to go along with this. What is the very last effects you'd want to acquire via those moves?

Of direction, it is probably to grow to be a amazing philosopher, however why do you want to turn out to be a powerful philosopher? Where will it take you in your existence? How will you and those round you advantage from this incoming alternate in your lifestyles?

This is achieved first as a manner to growth the incentive on the way to go through the last 9 steps with the rigor you'll need to succeed.

Action Steps

On a piece of paper, write down the following 6 commands: Physical fitness, Emotional fitness, Family & Friends, Career, Personal Finances, and Faith.

Take a non-public stock of in which you experience as despite the fact that you stand in each of these instructions. What are you glad with, what are you unhappy with?

Now, determine what final outcomes you need from each of the 6 instructions. Write effects for a 10 years into the destiny, a 5 years into the destiny, and a 1 12 months into the future (long time, mid time period, and short time period). Keep in thoughts that the handiest obstacles you'll be putting on yourself aren't necessarily real, they will be certainly obstacles that you've determined on.

Regardless of what's written here, you need to recognize that splendid questioning gets you there.

Reflection

Why are we able to use the phrase "final results" right here in area of "cause"? It is due to the fact irrespective of what, you may attain an final results, whether or not that very last outcomes is excessive great or bad.

When we decide on what our final results may be, unexpectedly the entirety turns into greater smooth due to the fact understanding your results for each of the 6 categories will help popularity your thoughts on what your desires are.

## Chapter 12: Conduct a Self-Inventory

Conduct an honest self-inventory of your mind, feelings, and subjects which might be critical to you.

Do no longer be discouraged, bored, put off, or circulate slowly, on your achievement and happiness are at stake. Keep your mind centered at the various blessings you may enjoy if you gain your intention.

This first step calls for your full interest and cooperation. You want to ensure that the whole lot will hold in line with your motive.

Action Steps

Choose a private region and the proper time to have a study yourself with out distraction. You can also use a pocket ebook to list down matters approximately your self.

In one area, list down what you truly assume are your high-quality tendencies or recurring mind. In some other vicinity, list down the horrible ones. Just use key phrases for simplicity. Place similar dispositions or mind underneath one class.

Examples of superb tendencies are friendliness, helpfulness, generosity, honesty, and overall performance. Examples of terrible traits are selfishness, laziness, disrespect, lying, and dishonesty. Thoughts hold from tendencies. This exercising will attempt to reform terrible thoughts and inclinations into great ones.

Reflection

Changing one's outlook or manner of questioning first requires expertise oneself as an extended manner as feasible. Recognize your strengths and weaknesses honestly and objectively. You do no longer have to finish the self-stock in a unmarried sitting, despite the fact that. Your preference to reap achievement and to be glad will encourage you to carry out this step, even if you locate it tough on the start.

## Chapter 13: Determine the Causes

The great of your life is the outstanding of the questions you ask. For steps 3 and 4, we're asking the question "Why?". More specially, we're asking "Why are these poor developments a part of who I am at this point in time?" By asking this query, we can start to see what the actual reasons for those tendencies are. Once those motives were decided, we will then learn how to correct them.

Negative mind and tendencies will ultimately get replaced with their excessive terrific equivalents. Self-self guarantee will replace shyness. Friendliness will update hostility. Trust will replace mistrust. You must hint the ones motives and listing them down.

If you are shy, you may be too aware of your lack of abilities. You might also additionally moreover have suffered disappointments or rejection inside the past. If you mistrust others, it is probably because of the reality a person crucial led you to just accept as true with some thing that wasn't actual. If you're habitually irritable or quarrelsome, you could enjoy insecure and protective approximately some thing in you.

If you have a tendency to criticize others privately or publicly, you could feel small about your self. Putting others down makes you revel in larger. If you're competitive, it may advocate you be afflicted by a experience of powerlessness. If you're vulgar collectively along with your speech or seems, it can be due to the fact you lack self-apprehend.

Replacing bad thinking with splendid wondering is similar to a scientific evaluation. You want to find out the cause of the hassle first, you then discover the remedy for the bothered scenario.

Action Steps

After you have got indexed down all your terrible trends or mind along your notable ones inside the previous step, make the effort to determine the real reasons you continue to harbor such terrible tendencies or mind. Look returned on all of your existence studies that introduced about you to harbor such thoughts thus far. Ask your self if it's miles no matter the fact that vital if you want to maintain right now to the pain and/or humiliation because of the ones stories or if you need to ultimately flow into on from them on the identical time as however maintaining to coronary coronary coronary heart the treasured commands you determined out from them.

Reflection

The most effective powerful remedy for a disorder is the detection of the cause. Only then can the treatment be accomplished or devised. Doctors are specially skilled to make diagnoses and to prescribe treatments. In this example, you are your very personal psychologist. If you're sincere enough, you can discover your personal problems.

It is neither clean nor exceptional to appearance indoors ourselves for weak spot. Often, it makes us lose vanity. But with self-honesty, humility, and a actual preference for improvement, you could do it like an professional.

## Chapter 14: Your Participation

No bad emotion or belief can input your mind and affect you without your permission. Unfortunately, despite the fact that, maximum humans are very touchy to concept. We are all raised to are looking for the approval of others. What human beings say can be very influential to our self-view, notwithstanding the truth that their opinion human beings is not true.

This is why many human beings go to incredible lengths simply to get approval from others. A pat on the returned and a nod are very effective system that may make or break us. It is consequently tragic that other human beings absolutely dictate what and the way we want to be or behave. What is even extra tragic is that we allow them to do it to us.

You are in fact an energetic player in the formation of your poor dispositions and mind. People can best skip as far as propose; your response comes to a choice what takes place to their idea. You can decide to reject their bad idea. You can determine to experience first rate about yourself.

The final purpose of horrible questioning and mind-set is being unaware that you can clearly manipulate what enters your thoughts. People haven't any energy over your choice. You are the simplest selection-maker in your internal global. In a actual way, you pick out to be sad and unsuccessful.

Action Steps

After creating a phrase of your lousy dispositions or thoughts similarly to the existence studies that precipitated you to harbor them inside the first location, you may be conscious that each one of them have one detail in common—they remain for your reminiscence thus far due to the fact you allow them to. Not pretty, how one-of-a-kind human beings see you—whether proper or not—had a hand in making this take location. Still, you allowed yourself to be swayed thru the use of fantastic people's views of you that it affected your non-public view of your self.

Do your incredible to find out what it's far that reasons human beings to mention such subjects approximately you further to why you're letting their views of you have got an impact on the way you live your existence. Are you searching out their approval? Do you want to belong to a specific enterprise? Or do you honestly desire for others no longer to emblem you as someone to be ridiculed? Whatever it is, you should understand that what others consider you need to now not decide your happiness. But earlier than you figure on being extra assertive and not letting others dictate your actions, you first need to realize what exactly are the proscribing perspectives that others have of you—views that you have allowed to steer your mind and actions all this time.

Reflection

We are added up with the eye that lovely others is what is going to make us "proper." Social approval has been the conventional desired for reputation. However, times have modified. People in the meanwhile are more massive-minded and new approaches of questioning have prevailed.

One of these techniques is first-rate questioning. Today's people are inclined to understand others' right to turn out to be what they want. More and further people are enlightened. There is a heightened emphasis on independence. You are privileged to were born into this age.

## Chapter 15: Disconnect

Now that you have observed or exposed the reasons of your bad thoughts and tendencies, you may decide to save you giving in to them. Yes, you could! Remember that your mind are YOUR thoughts. You are in complete manipulate of them, irrespective of how strongly others propose them to you.

If you have got were given been shy all your life due to a ailment or failure, you can prevent feeding the notion that the contamination or failure makes you small. Remember which you are the most effective one which makes all the options interior you. One or a few or perhaps many defects or screw ups need no longer make you enjoy small. It can be other people's favored of self-judgment, however you can reject that famous.

The choice to disconnect from the recommendations might be a large victory for you. It is a high detail in growing a cutting-edge manner of questioning sincerely about yourself. Positive questioning will make you break free from shyness and specific poor tendencies. It will set you loose to end up a modern day man or woman.

Always recall that human nature resists exchange. Initiating alternate on my own calls for terrific internal electricity and concern. Sustaining the way calls for even greater power and place. Determination is the splendid function of a few, however it is also the fundamental element of fulfillment and freedom from the clutches of horrible questioning.

A first taste of fulfillment will excite you, but it can moreover make you slide lower back. It is as tough as mountain climbing a mountain— the higher you circulate, the more the warfare. One slip or fall might also moreover even discourage you. It ought to make you feel that all your efforts are useless. But consider which you do now not attain the peak of a mountain after taking only a few steps.

Substituting amazing wondering for terrible wondering is just like scaling a mountain. You skip in the direction of the pull of gravity within the shape of the natural resistance to trade. Only courage and determination will let you attain the peak. The same goes for reaching a pleasant questioning sample and thoughts-set.

Action Steps

If for now not whatever else, being aware of different human beings's opinion of you and the way they experience you want to act will assist you apprehend that there are exceptional extra splendid and extra powerful strategies of motivating your self. You start thru sincerely acknowledging that what others enjoy is right for you isn't continually going to take you a protracted manner in life. Besides, they do no longer stand to benefit from it—besides, probable, by means of manner of drawing a few delight from being able to get you to act as they wish. Obviously, you should no longer deliver them this pleasure.

After you've got were given positioned out that you can pick out out to put a forestall to your horrible thinking, you will possibly have hassle knowing wherein to start. Remember that self-inventory you finished earlier? Go via all the notable tendencies or thoughts which you have written down and see which of them need to serve as perfect leap-off elements on your adventure in the direction of making first-rate wondering a every day dependancy.

For example, in case you indexed friendliness as one in every of your immoderate best inclinations, you could consider sports in which you may workout in addition developing this trait, collectively with doing volunteer paintings in your free time. As long as your motive is to genuinely assist specific people out or to make new buddies and not definitely to are seeking out others' approval, it's going to probably be much less complex that permits you to make a addiction out of being great. And because of the fact you're making a dependancy out of striving to impart your positivity on to others by means of being pleasant, you amplify the addiction of wonderful questioning as nicely.

Regardless of your chosen trait soar-off aspect, this exercising can help you boom the habit of extremely good questioning with the beneficial aid of focusing for your present day-day strengths. Simply positioned, it's lots much less complicated to artwork on what you're already genuine at in vicinity of racking your brain looking to consider what else you will be suitable at.

After you have got got solidified and labored thru that first trait, maintain going and examine the same approach for all of the one-of-a-type trends!

Reflection

Society devised a manner to make certain peace and order with the aid of manner of infusing the want for social approval amongst people, but it went too an extended way as putting itself as a popular of conduct. Everyone fears social rejection. Hence, humans internalize social norms as internal censors. Its restrictive and punitive nature has added on a good deal sadness.

Although conventional values and prejudices die hard, contemporary concept has step by step driven them away. You can also moreover now have an amazing time a brand new openness amongst an increasing number of people. Tolerance and recognition of person versions have become the order of the day.

## Chapter 16: Human Nature and Self-Understanding

Although no personalities are completely alike, the dynamics of human nature is regular. We all have not unusual desires. Everyone wants to sense important regardless of his faults. We all need to be reputable. We need to be heard.

No one desires to be disregarded. We all need to be successful. We all need to be favored further to cherished for what we are. Success makes us entire and essential. Nothing makes us that better than achievement.

A understanding of human nature will supply an motive of why certain humans behave the manner they do. It may additionally even permit you to recognise why you behave as you do. Therefore, gaining knowledge of about human nature lets in you realize and apprehend yourself better. It makes you notice that you aren't by myself to your troubles.

At the equal time, data of human nature allows you understand others. Many of your terrible emotions and thinking about the ones people can burn up in case you apprehend them. You will no longer only have the functionality to triumph over your bitter mind approximately different human beings; you may additionally win them once more if they'll be willing.

Action Steps

As you find out your strengths and weaknesses and generally exercise the habits that lead you to excessive great thinking, you will gain a higher data of why humans—yourself covered—suppose and act the manner they do. As you exercise your preferred behavior that will help you become a awesome philosopher, be aware of the differences to your mind and actions. Compare who you're now to who you had been before on the same time as poor thinking have turn out to be nonetheless a dependancy for you. As you maintain in thoughts the matters about you that led you to adopt horrific thinking in advance than, you'll understand what to avoid within the future so that you will in no way all another time fall into that trap.

At the equal time, as you determine your newfound conduct that result in exceptional questioning, you can extra with out problem discover any modifications on your person that enabled you to efficaciously undertake the ones behavior. What features or methods of wondering did you start schooling to make those changes viable? What did you need to surrender to make way for those? Your answers to the ones questions will characteristic your guide in keeping your development in case you another time discover your self slipping or missing the incentive to transport ahead. What you have a look at from this workout additionally will let you apprehend people, even people who aren't striving to make great thinking part of their everyday dwelling.

Reflection

Knowledge becomes strength in this example due to the fact you practice it in your particular conditions. Others have the same dreams as you do. They make the same errors as you do. They want to be as glad and a hit as you do. They have thriller pains and the desire to conquer as you do.

Knowing why humans behave in positive strategies locations you in control of your bad questioning and thoughts-set. That is actual power—over yourself! And your conduct will trade as your questioning and mind-set alternate from horrible to effective.

## Chapter 17: Discover and Understand Your Own Emotional Needs

Whether you want it or no longer, your feelings rule you some distance more than your mind does. It is not the mind that makes most of your alternatives however what you enjoy. Changing your way of wondering from terrible to excessive high-quality method searching greater into your feelings. You can be in deep want of hobby, approval, forgiveness, or recognize.

The problem with maximum people is they deny their internal most emotional hurts and desires. These hurts may be "forgotten" responses to three far off experience. They can be too painful to widely known, so they may be buried deep within the subconscious mind in our mental garbage can. However, because of the truth they will be no longer confronted and solved, they come decrease returned to dangle-out and control you.

No experience is ever honestly forgotten. Being human, you pick the whole lot and all of us based to your feeling in vicinity of on your mind or reason. And considering no longer all of us is aware of or is acquainted with how hurts can harm one's conceitedness, you could don't forget what number of unfortunate stories are buried deep in the unconscious!

It is consequently small surprise why very many human beings are terrible thinkers. Those unresolved pains urge for recovery. They scream for restoration in a single-of-a-type workplace paintings, typically as safety mechanisms. You may be subconsciously showing your uneasiness in the form of horrific wondering. Others who assume they will be satisfactory thinkers may moreover furthermore handiest be the usage of it to control.

We all starvation to talk our mind and coronary coronary heart, however as stated in advance, cussed, traditional social norms inhibit and limit us from freely expressing ourselves. People provide their nod of approval to the kid or person who is pliable whilst honesty is taken into consideration rise up.

Nevertheless, your desire to speak out and be yourself often deviates from the tips. Besides, human nature will itself stress you to bolt out. Like rivers, nature will generally attempting to find to level up. The ache of irritability, sadness, anger, worry, or hostility will disturb you until it's miles expressed and solved. Hiding or misrepresenting what you simply feel will simplest make subjects worse.

Feelings are responses to situations. Nature endowed you with individuals who permits you to defend you from damage. They are really properly, consequently. Self-protection is its purpose. It can first-class be unacceptable whilst expressed or realized in dangerous or unlawful tactics.

Action Steps

The previous step confirmed you ways better self-records ends in greater popularity of your prevailing developments that cause super thinking. Another direct impact of this is that you emerge as greater aware of what is to your coronary coronary heart in addition to what you really need to acquire as an individual.

With each concept or action that comes in your mind, make it a dependancy to ask your self: "Will doing this movement or harboring this belief genuinely assist me get to in which I want to be?" To apprehend the answer to that question, you need to go deep internal yourself and study your feelings, including your first-rate dreams further in your most painful hurts. Acknowledge them and make a conscious attempt to address them in vicinity of actually relegating them to the corners of your thoughts.

Remember that exquisite thinking moreover includes acknowledging your actual self. You can't have a super outlook in lifestyles if you comprehend deep in your coronary heart that you are denying yourself the liberty to specific the manner you in reality revel in and the possibility to ease or completely eliminate your ache.

Reflection

Human beings are more feeling than wondering beings. We clearly experience greater than we expect. Feelings compel us to do subjects that our personal minds may want to in any other case now not approve of, but that is what human nature is. Yet feelings are there to protect you, not offer you with a tough time.

Understanding your personal feelings will prevent you from channeling them in risky or unrealistic techniques. That is why the notable truth seeker says that the number one distinctive feature is self-knowledge. You cannot impose fantastic wondering on your self in case you want to cover up an unsightly feeling. Refrain from condemning yourself.

## Chapter 18: Support Sources

In replacing a horrible thinking sample and mind-set with satisfactory ones, you'll want experts or the ones who've succeeded inside the challenge. They can be your counselor, pastor, a psychologist, a lecturer-expert, or an older and wiser individual. Their store of knowledge and experience or know-how on human emotions is a veritable treasure chest.

You also can have a study extra books at the project or attend take a seat down-ins or lectures. The internet is full of authoritative assets on it, but be careful no longer to simply accept as true with all the statistics you find on line. Weigh what they'll be announcing and notice the way it applies to you.

Counselors and unique intellectual fitness specialists can be the maximum goal property of assist and idea. Still, an vintage relied on and informed buddy or pastor also can contribute treasured inputs as they apprehend your state of affairs better. Try combining the recommendation given to you by way of the usage of all of your belongings.

Pastors will clearly link your negative dispositions to religious thoughts. Mental fitness specialists will emphasize the medical thing. Your older friend can be subjective in giving advice. Each have to have cost.

Action Steps

In your journey toward becoming a pleasant truth seeker, part of statistics yourself and your feelings (as described inside the previous step) is knowing there are however areas where you'll probable stumble upon problem. This hassle ought to purpose you to slide short or without a doubt relapse into ordinary horrible thinking (as defined in step five), but this want to now not prevent you from persevering with to your journey. You've already made full-size profits thru this factor, so why prevent now?

No one ever said which you want to bypass it on my own. Fortunately, there are human beings to whom you could talk and ask questions on human emotions and a way to growth the addiction of powerful thinking. Look them up in the list or the internet. Set an appointment together along with your university counselor. Your church's pastor may be approached after a issuer. Mental health professionals can be available in precise facilities with the beneficial resource of appointment. And your older and smart pal may additionally additionally moreover first-rate be a cellphone call away.

All consultations with the above need to be extremely good. Be as direct, easy, and amiable as feasible. You want help to put off what receives in the way of you turning into a exquisite logician. Let them understand that.

You also can need to method your mother and father if you expect they'll be able to apprehend you, however there are instances that they may be the prohibitive motives of your horrific trends. It is higher that you are trying to find advice from someone who's more goal.

Do no longer hesitate to are searching for recommendation from others in case you are unsure approximately what you found or have observe. Ask for clarifications and further recommendation. You will be surprised and enjoy extensively relieved to discover that your situation isn't in any respect precise. When you start to understand your self, you're on the manner to controlling your life.

Reflection

Many human beings had been there and executed that, so the announcing is going. They are important property of concept and guidance to you. Find out how they received their respective battles. Discover their pitfalls and strengths. Great humans are great now not due to the reality they're born amazing; they've got come to be excellent due to the fact they overcame extraordinary battles.

They also are property of energy at the identical time as you fall again and again all over again. Many battles aren't acquired as soon as, and it does no longer make you less treasured a person just due to the fact you fail and fail all all over again. What is crucial is that you upward thrust with every fall.

Do not worry failure or disappointment. They will commonly accompany all venture and struggle. Fix your sight for your reason of fulfillment and happiness. Change your mind-set toward disappointments and disasters. No one will do it for you besides you.

Also don't forget that notable you could set your limits on your dream. As stated in advance, you are the only choice-maker in your universe. You can limit or reject what others say or recollect you. Your individual is your nation.

## Chapter 19: The Golden Rule

Positive questioning and attitude are based on what's actual and what's proper; that is the great which means that of "brilliant." Many human beings do not forget that being unoffensive, always smiling and being high-quality, and doing favors will cause them to splendid thinkers. It has cost simplest if it has a moral basis.

Being splendid isn't always similar to or a alternative to being accurate, even though. Many times, you have to be ugly an excellent manner to produce a extremely good impact. Always comply with the Golden Rule: "Do unto others as you may have them do unto you." Thus, your behavior is your positive guide to the manner you want others to act inside the path of you.

You need no longer be too spiritual to turn out to be absolutely excessive pleasant. However, many religious texts from the vital religions across the area screen that that could be a positive manual to becoming honest. And whilst you are sincere, you are at the right path to turning into simply first-class. You turn out to be a real strain of proper to your self and to others.

Action Steps

There are not any specific actions to be taken underneath this step other than being honest and honest in all of your dealings and letting this come to be a dependancy in itself. When you continuously try and uphold the truth even in your most effective moves, it turns into an awful lot much less complex that allows you to look subjects as they virtually are and tell it like it's miles. By assessment, having to rack your mind considering some thing that you are feeling other humans would really like to concentrate becomes more tough, for this reason making it tons a whole lot much less and plenty much less possible for you as a direction of movement over time.

Reflection

You do no longer want to cognizance or intention perfection if you want to advantage success or happiness. You start with the truth and take delivery of it. It can be ugly however it all depends on your thoughts-set. You can change that mindset right now.

You can come to be a really exquisite truth seeker most effective on honest and suitable grounds. Being tremendous isn't always a replacement. Begin by way of being actual to your self and make the important corrections for your horrible trends the effective manner. Then you will be in your way to becoming a sincerely fantastic logician.

## Chapter 20: Influence on Others

The thing approximately fantastic questioning is that it's far a dependancy that everybody have to exercise whether or no longer they're rich or terrible, informed or uneducated, fans of a selected religion or now not aligned with any religion in any respect, and so on. Thus, it makes great revel in to educate humans approximately it and to inspire them to comprise it of their every day lives, especially if their addiction of terrible thinking is inflicting all of them styles of problems.

One of the quality techniques of coaching human beings approximately incredible wondering is to exercise it your self. You need to take every opportunity to show others what terrific questioning can help them attain.

Action Steps

By this time, you may have already made nice questioning a every day dependancy. You have taken to coronary coronary heart all which you have observed and as a result, it comes smooth to you. The subsequent step is to use your every day interactions with one-of-a-kind humans to show them the manner to head approximately it.

When you speak, you need to be an agent of reality, honesty, and objectivity. When you explicit your views, you have to deliver others the possibility to precise theirs as well. When you cope with tough humans or conditions, you want to exert try and recollect feasible answers in location of living on the impediments you face. And if you have started out a top notch dependancy, preserve practising it so that everyone can see what they'll advantage through consistency.

Reflection

Teaching people about summary concepts can most effective obtain this lots. You should be willing to expose them what they want to understand with the aid of using way of your personal instance. In doing so, you moreover mght in addition increase your very own existing fantastic wondering addiction, so that you at once enjoy the workout as nicely.

## Chapter 21: What Is a Positive Mind?

If you want to have a effective mind, it is crucial to understand what a awesome mind seems like first. How are you capable of gain your purpose if you don't apprehend what the cause is in the first area? Obviously, a effective thoughts is one that looks on the intense element, attempts to find the diamonds inside the coal, and isn't always aspect tracked with the beneficial resource of obstacles or the terrible reviews of others. That stated, a immoderate excellent mind can't reject the horrible elements of existence each because of the fact the excellent and horrible elements want to be in balance. Balance is one of the maximum crucial factors of life. A excellent thoughts is also not a mind that takes us to a nation of "magical thinking". Yes, you need to have a high-quality outlook and keep away from matters that sluggish you down, but no, you can't truly reject a few element due to the fact you don't like it or because it does now not healthful your mold.

This sounds a bit counter intuitive, however think about this: rejection is negativity.

Adding negativity to negativity makes extra negativity! Two wrongs don't make a right as they're saying. For example, if you are an athlete who without a doubt ran a mile and your train informed you that you have been sluggish, you may do three topics. First, you can suppose, "That train is so terrible; he need to be incorrect because of the reality I'm already super." Second, you could assume, "Well, I bet because of this I need to get better." Third, you may assume, "The teach is right; I will never run faster." The first alternative rejected the awful criticism however created a scenario in which there has been no room to exercising more difficult, and consequently, no way to get better. The 2nd choice normal the bad complaint however created a tremendous mind-set— this is, to hold transferring forward. The 1/three desire traditional the horrific criticism but took it too far, making it way greater horrible than what it genuinely turned into in the first place. The athlete who decided on the primary opportunity isn't going to win any medals considering that they already count on they'll be incredible. This is unrealistic, and as a surrender end result, he's going to haven't any room to extend and stay on the identical degree. The zero.33 preference is sincerely as awful due to the reality the athlete emerge as short to without a doubt take delivery of it and give up; therefore, he gained't be getting any higher both! That said, the athlete who is privy to they may be capable of get higher has the handiest attitude, and to be able to lead him to getting higher and higher through the years.

This thoughts-set is so essential, now not most effective for sports activities sports activities however moreover for the entirety. The mind-set of knowing that there may be room to enhance might be the single most essential thoughts-set that someone also can have. This is the way wherein all first rate human beings come to be extremely good at whatever they do, and it's far known as "a amateur's thoughts". Someone with a beginner's mind must have 50 years of enjoy, however they will be generally thinking "What can I take a look at nowadays?" or "What must I exercise?" or "What does this random person understand that I do now not?"

Always do your super to remain humble, and attempt to examine and make bigger in every scenario which you input into in existence. The super way to maintain a exceptional thoughts is to hold your mind open. Allow new thoughts in and don't forget them for some time in advance than making a decision the manner you enjoy about them. Also, pay attention to what subjects experience like: in the event that they feel right, explore them, and if no longer, avoid them.

Essentially, I am asking you to behave like a little one for the relaxation of your life! A infant is constantly studying subjects, and fine, babies cry and emerge as upset, but all of us is aware about that a toddler is happy as long as their smooth dreams are met. No one ever sees a toddler and thinks "Wow, what an boastful toddler, that baby thinks they apprehend everything!" A newbie's mind is an thoughts-set on the way to in no way come to be obsolete so long as you're alive. There is a cause that babies are born this manner; that is, a beginner's thoughts is the superb way to have a look at and develop and beautify in every problem of existence. Having this intellectual thoughts-set can even routinely make your thoughts more exceptional due to the truth you'll not be judging topics or searching out what makes them inferior. Instead, you can take a look at the sector and find out the things that assist you come to be better, and nothing feels better than constantly improving.

The amateur's thoughts is an instance of stability. Balance may be the unmarried most important difficulty of a positive thoughts nation. Modern psychology and treatment are commonly seeking to assist human beings emerge as greater balanced in frame and in thoughts. Many subjects impact balance, however your inner balance is ultimately something that you by myself manipulate. Other things impact it, but simplest you may control it! This isn't typically easy because of the fact balance isn't an area, but as an opportunity, it's far a method. For example, the swinging pendulum of an antique university clock is perfectly balanced: it swings to at the least one aspect after which back to the alternative. It does receives stuck on one thing, and it does no longer forestall moving as long as the clock is going for walks. Of path, we aren't first rate like a clock. Sometimes, we get stuck on one aspect or the opposite, and occasionally, we surely prevent moving the least bit for some time. But because you want to have a greater amazing mind, it is time to investigate a few tool to help you pass in that course!

Let's think about the tale of Goldilocks. She wanders into the residence of a family of bears and well-knownshows three bowls of porridge. One bowl is genuinely too heat, one is truely too cold, and one is honestly right. When you encounter subjects in existence, you can react in those three techniques. "Too heat" is anger, rejection, violence, aggression, or jealously. "Too cold" is unhappiness, giving up, melancholy, bending over, or thinking that it is able to in no manner be you except. These extremes are virtually the equal factor in a manner. "Too warm" is pushing the feelings out of doors onto different people, at the same time as "too cold" is pulling the ones same feelings internal and questioning the problem is constantly you. "Just right" is the steadiness of the 2: it is reputation, improvement, emulation, exercise, and reading.

Why don't more human beings act this way? For one component, it's miles an awful lot much less hard to find the extreme aspects of "too cold" and "too warm" due to the fact everyone can feel in which the extremes are thinking about the reality that they may be as a long way as they will be capable of skip! "Just proper" is more difficult to hold because locating the center is a everyday technique. It is a manner in that you are continuously swimming, searching, analyzing, and growing. You can not anticipate to be super because of the reality you will always be upset. Why? ...because of the truth satisfactory isn't genuinely viable. However, if you count on to research and exchange, then you may be glad every day because of the truth this is some issue that you could do for the relaxation of your existence. Even if you lived to be one thousand years antique!

The novice's mind and the equipment provided inside the ebook are truly trendy. I advocate that you comply with this book to the give up and take a look at the gear as they're provided right proper right here. However, as time is going on, you could constantly adapt those gadget to different factors of existence. Any new undertaking or challenge will advantage from stability and a newbie's thoughts. That said, happiness and fulfillment starts offevolved within, so have a look at this via and use it on your thoughts first because of the fact as speedy because the thoughts is in perfect balance, then the whole lot else will look at definitely!

## Chapter 22: Starting a Positive Cycle

The prison suggestions of physics say that an item at relaxation has a bent to live at relaxation, but an object in motion has a tendency to stay in motion. In precise terms, if you start shifting then you may preserve moving, however if you stay although, then you definately obtained't float in any respect. Sometimes, human beings don't pass due to the truth they are afraid of making a mistake or transferring within the incorrect direction. This is not unusual thinking, but it is not surely real. Think approximately this: if you are moving, you may alternate route on every occasion you need to. This is why you received't hesitate any in addition to get began out; mistakes are not disasters but as an opportunity methods to observe as you begin to look at the newbie's mind. This bankruptcy will train you a way to get a pleasing cycle going, which absolutely motives your mind to rewire itself right into a extra top notch state. The process can on occasion be a touch hard, however this financial ruin teaches you a way to get going and the manner to have amusing along the way.

All too often, we listen people talking approximately terrible cycles, along with addiction. We have all heard approximately how those begin as small troubles but fast snowball into very horrible conditions. But that is first-rate half of of of the story! Why is it that we don't pay attention approximately exceptional cycles? Successful humans of a substantial range have excessive exceptional cycles, but perhaps, they're so busy being a fulfillment that they don't stop and speak about it! Today, we're able to speak approximately it and display you the manner to get it commenced. Everyone needs a few assist and a few steerage on this technique because of the truth going from being despite the fact that to being in motion may be jarring and tough every now and then. This is ordinary, and if you revel in the ones feelings, certainly remind your self that this is a part of the manner. Due to this truth, it is useful to make this procedure a laugh for yourself at the same time as you are doing it, to help you to get stimulated and to help you hold going.

In the very last 10 years or so, a today's word has emerged into the English language:

"gamification" (said "activity-a-fication"). This word refers to the software program of recreation layout to additives of actual lifestyles. And nowadays, you begin to practice this technological understand-a way for your non-public thoughts! This isn't anything new—at the identical time as a toddler is given a sweet for completing their chores, that could be a form of gamification. Gamification frames an modern element as a sport, in order that it motivates you to art work and makes the work more a laugh. You will take a look at this for your intellectual mind-set to make starting a outstanding cycle fun!

Start to play this undertaking as often as you can. Right when you go out a situation, any mundane scenario, do not forget the whole lot that emerge as stated. Think approximately the entirety they stated to you and the entirety you said in go back. It's good enough if you can't recollect the precise words, but be sincere about what it felt like. Now reflect onconsideration on your reactions—changed into it "too warm", "too bloodless", or "honestly proper"? These may be diffused emotions, so it's ok if you don't realize the answers. Just bypass without delay to the following element and ask yourself the question over again—become it "too hot", "too cold", or "honestly right"?

This game is one in which there may be simplest one manner to win: keep playing the sport. That is because of the fact the greater you ask your self this easy query, the more with out hassle you can solution it. Just be sincere approximately how topics revel in, and you'll enhance regularly time beyond law. Don't worry approximately retaining score—simply ask if it have become "too warm", "too bloodless", or "just proper". This easy sport permits you spot your self, see the way you act, and beautify your actions through the years. Even in case you sense stupid or out of area doing this, simply preserve going! Scientists now say that your very own body doesn't apprehend the difference amongst when you stress a smile or even because it takes place spontaneously. That technique that during case you just start being what you want to emerge as, you becomes what you need to be through the years. Just maintain going! If you make a decision to this method, you may change for the better, so start utilizing this undertaking to your every day interactions in recent times.

It is said that many folks that live to be extra than a hundred years vintage have a completely regular healthy dietweight-reduction plan and way of life. I am not pronouncing you want to devour the equal detail every day, however you do need to have a everyday exercise in case you want to get better. In this case, in reality interest on gambling this little hobby some instances an afternoon and ensure which you do it each day. Rewiring the mind right into a greater fine kingdom takes time, so hold going even if you don't enjoy a trade right away. Commit to an entire week of gambling this recreation each day! The maximum crucial detail is that you surely hold going!

## Chapter 23: Keeping the Ball Rolling

The toughest detail is getting started out. That's great because of the truth you are already doing that, and now, we flow into to the subsequent detail—maintaining that high-quality cycle rolling. Remember that that is a method, and even though it gets less tough over time, it furthermore lasts a long term. You will flow up and down, have days which might be better than others, and additionally virtually fail to be in a first rate kingdom at times too. All of this stuff aren't first-rate ordinary however furthermore certainly critical. This is the way you examine, and you're now training a more fantastic you. The exceptional human beings within the worldwide, whether or not or not in sports activities sports, industrial enterprise, or any hassle of existence, do no longer start off on the pinnacle of their difficulty. Everyone has to exercise. You even needed to exercising how to talk and the manner to have a look at. In reality, in case you are studying this, then you definately need to have practiced pretty masses! It's clearly that you had been probable too younger to keep in mind doing it. This is proof which you already have the whole lot which you need to have each day— a an increasing number of high-quality mind.

Remember: "Hard art work beats capabilities while competencies refuses to artwork." In splendid terms, it doesn't depend quantity how well you are at this little game so long as keep playing it. So, why is it that humans begin such a lot of factors however turn out to be now not completing them? It is because of how they react to the subjects that display up to them. How commonly has a person informed you "I grow to be going to \_\_\_\_\_ until \_\_\_\_\_ befell to me"? When life throws up an impediment, we're capable of permit it save you us or whilst can discover a new path! This economic catastrophe is all about retaining the ball rolling, so at the same time as a few thing massive and frightening comes up in advance of you, surely flip and go with the flow round it! It is adequate to trade path, it's far ok to fail, and it's far good enough to be wrong occasionally. But you need to hold moving if you need to move everywhere!

It is also very critical to apprehend what your reason is, to make that intention crystal clean, and to remind yourself of that aim all that factor. It enables to pick out a aim this is low fee, one sentence prolonged, and easy to recollect. Here is a remarkable aim to have, "Every day I create a greater wonderful mind." Simple, quick, and excellent are the way to move. Say this to yourself each time you have a threat; although it feels regular or untrue at the start, it will become proper because the method rolls on.

Here is some specific beneficial trick to begin the use of proper now. These days, the top athletes in the global use visualization as an critical part of their schooling. If you are training to win a race, you run every day, consume wholesome, and you visualize on your thoughts the real second wherein you pass your fighters and damage through the end line ahead of truely all and sundry else. Right now, you may stop analyzing for a 2nd, near your eyes, and recall your thoughts turning into a extra excessive excellent, mild-filled region. See It lights up with excellent slight. Try it now. You can do that little workout at any time, even in case you only have three seconds to spare. Again, it is able to seem untrue in advance than the whole thing, or you may see nice a tiny mild or no slight in any respect. This is ideal sufficient. Your thoughts, your body, and your mind try a few issue new, so it can take commonly in advance than this is natural. Just hold the ball rolling. Now, near your eyes all once more and notice your mind lights up with super colourful mild.

How did that experience? Try it a third time proper now. Was that any remarkable? This little visualization exercising is just like the use of a bicycle. It may moreover take often to end up natural, however it's miles going to be yours for the rest of your lifestyles! And don't forget that you are changing your own mind for the higher, and the extra you workout, the greater you could improvement.

Now, take a second to recollect those very last chapters and be privy to the three method you've got already got—asking if it became "too hot", "too bloodless", or "just right"; reminding yourself of your clean one-sentence intention; and visualizing a mind full of great light. It is so crucial which you use these little techniques each day, and if you bypass over a day, don't be anxious! Just maintain going and keep in mind that that could be a recreation you win as long as you preserve gambling!

## Chapter 24: Jumping over Traps and Pitfalls

You can continuously come another time and re-have a look at this e book each time you enjoy which you need some steering or motivation. This ebook is designed that will help you come to be a happier you, so keep it close to and allow it help you as often as you want. Sometimes, all of us need to be reminded of the things we already knew, however forget about approximately over the years. This is normal, and there is no disgrace in looking back over what you have got were given already study. No disgrace, exceptional gain!

As we observed in advance than, you'll typically have setbacks, instances you were wrong, and disregarded possibilities to get higher. That is proper sufficient, that is normal, and that is some element that everybody will face. However, that doesn't suggest which you want to jump straight away into each awful situation or slam head first into every impediment. Part of preserving a great cycle rolling is being able to roll right beyond as many obstacles as you may, and this financial disaster will give you provide gear that will help you stay on path. Always undergo in thoughts that barriers, setbacks, and pain are everyday.

Remember that we're looking to have a beginner's thoughts, like a baby. Babies take a look at and increase every day, but toddlers additionally get hurt, get uncomfortable, and cry all of the time. The more you could get keep of that there can be setbacks, pain, and traumatic conditions, the extra resultseasily you could float beyond them. In remarkable terms, as you take shipping of hassle, you turns into happier and further splendid through the years. Someone who buys a lottery rate tag watching for to win may be disappointed masses or masses of times earlier than they win. However, a person who buys a lottery fee price ticket looking earlier to not some thing can super be happy once they win and will revel in surely ordinary after they do now not. The recreation of turning into greater first-rate is a lot like this in a few techniques. Expect which you are not playing a recreation of threat now. You are playing a activity of ability! This approach that as you exercise being balanced and having a novice's thoughts, the sport will become a whole lot much less difficult to play and your thoughts becomes greater wonderful. There is not any hazard involved, simplest the attempt you're making to continue gambling.

As you examine the 3 techniques from the final chapters (asking the query, repeating your aim, and visualizing a high remarkable thoughts), you becomes greater nice. But the arena out of doors of you may essentially be the same. This approach that the identical antique boundaries of existence will although present themselves, and you could regardless of the reality that ought to come upon them. The exceptional manner to deal with that is to move spherical those conflicts in advance than they come to be actual problems. However, you moreover may additionally need to make sure that you are concerned in as many excessive quality situations as you in all likelihood can! When a state of affairs is beginning, ask yourself the way it feels. Your thoughts is already first-rate at seeing the location as it must be, but every so often, anybody forget about approximately about to invite it to do its interest. You may even simply truly ask the question from the previous chapters, truly change it so that it applies to the scenario round you. If the state of affairs is "too warmness", it can experience risky, irritated, too active, unpredictable, or unstable. If the scenario is "too bloodless", it is able to enjoy completely risk-free, depressed, clearly snug, haven't any movement, or have no capability to expand. These are the two fashionable forms of boundaries in lifestyles. Both of them purpose you to waste your strength and time: one makes you run round and do topics which may be useless, whilst the possibility reasons you to stay in one location and in no way exchange.

But a few matters are not limitations the least bit, but rather conditions that let you beautify. These are the locations, regions, and people you need to surround yourself with. If a few issue is "surely right", it will feel uncomfortable but strong, difficult however strong, or perhaps dangerous however harmless. The secret Is too are seeking out out topics that purpose you to take a look at and to expand. And you must paintings to maintain stability on this approach. Jumping over the traps and pitfalls of lifestyles technique growing the discernment to peer topics as they in reality are and then deciding on what topics to jump into. Making errors is right enough so long as you operate every opportunity to investigate and enhance your method for the following time round. This is actual exceptional wondering, turning a setback into an possibility for increase and mastering! For example, a person who has in no way lifted weights earlier than does as many repetitions as viable with a heavy weight. They are extensively challenged however truly unstable. They moreover clearly emerge as hurting themselves and might not educate yet again, therefore dropping hundreds of electricity and time as they now need to heal. If the same person chooses to do only 3 repetitions with the lightest weight feasible, they may be surely secure but will now not be challenged at all. Even within the event that they preserve doing this each day, it will have no actual impact and they will basically stay the same all the time. If that person chooses a medium weight and does an less luxurious range of repetitions, they might hold going, experience challenged, and see actual increase and first-rate change over the years. Our mind is like this, undertaking it in less high-priced strategies as you method things with an open, newbie's thoughts. When a modern-day scenario or individual comes into your life, do your great to look at them with this query in thoughts. It isn't always vital to make your thoughts up proper now, as it may take time to research enough to reply the question. Just method with a novice's mind and undergo in thoughts that you may commonly alternate path while the need arises.

Now, examine this question to a few situations for your lifestyles currently, how do those conditions experience? The ones that fall into the "too heat" or "too cold" commands need to trade in some way. I can't say how or what due to the fact each state of affairs is specific, but actually test them honesty and ask if they're helping you. Are they clearly supporting you to develop? Are you reading some element from them? And are they developing the situations that lets in you to broaden a more wonderful thoughts? These are deep and personal questions, so ask yourself as truly and as honestly as you in all likelihood can.

Even the most dedicated and professional character will come across demanding conditions, so how do a achievement and remarkable people deal with these obstacles? They do their extremely good to hold a wonderful outlook and use every project to examine and to develop in something way that they could. Do no longer worry change, include it because of the reality the only aspect that does not trade is the truth that everything changes! Apply the query, remind your self of your purpose, and visualize the effective change for your thoughts. Now, you're already shifting in the proper direction!

## Chapter 25: Creating Success via Visualization

We've talked about what a high-quality thoughts is and a way to keep away from a number of the pitfalls as a way to hold you from having a incredible mind. Now it's time to talk approximately a few different important benefit of retaining a incredible mind. That gain is the power of visualization. By the usage of your wonderful thoughts to surround yourself in satisfactory mind and visualize success, you are much more likely to grow to be a fulfillment.

The manner this works is you visualize anything it's miles for your existence which you would like to be successful at. Whether it's a challenge, a carrying event, breaking a non-public awesome in the gym, walking a marathon, or what have you ever, imagining yourself doing properly is the first step inside the course of making it a truth. People who're greater assured in themselves are much more likely to achieve success. And self-self belief stems from having a pleasant thoughts.

Some examples of humans visualizing their manner to success include athletes who are envisioning triumphing a game or putting in an event, businesspeople who've made a sale or nailed a suggestion, or all and sundry who has labored their manner toward earning a promoting. Each of these conditions may be completed via visualizing achievement. Through tough art work and a first-rate outlook, you may be able to gain some component you put your thoughts to.

Take the athlete, as an example. Say they teach for the game of their preference each day of the week. Whether meaning going to the gymnasium for electricity education, walking to reinforce their cardiovascular stamina, or performing drills, the ones are only physical exercises. Physical carrying sports are fine half of the war. The specific half comes inside the form of intellectual education. Mental steering can be some issue from calming your nerves and moving into a nation of natural interest to imagining every and every movement you will take to be successful. The extra in-depth and unique your visualization is, the more likely you are to make that visualization into a truth.

Continuing alongside the athlete metaphor, say you are a baseball player. If you need to win a undertaking, you'll need to anticipate each movement you'll want to take to perform that. Think of everything that would seem over the route of a exercise and the manner you'll react to it. Once you've got got had been given your plan, preserve a terrific thoughts-set and turn it right into a fact. You'll be mentally prepared for anything is thrown at you and mentally sturdy enough to conform with via.

If in the end of this you're a bit skeptical, I don't blame you! However, research have proven that individuals who envision success are more likely to turn out to be a hit. Moreover, those who move over a normal mentally in advance than they comply with via bodily are more likely to preserve what they participated in. A take a look at following gymgoers had one organisation just visit the health club and training session, at the same time as the alternative institution went over their ordinary mentally first. The company that went over their habitual mentally showed higher muscle retention and ordinary extra effective outcomes.

So, no longer only does having a strong, outstanding thoughts hold you in real intellectual health, it can additionally maintain you in suitable physical health!

Start visualizing your way to fulfillment these days. The fantastic time to begin will constantly be the day past. The 2d exquisite time is these days. Don't preserve dwelling in remorse. Start as quickly as you awaken. Visualize your morning habitual, then noon, going into the early afternoon, and midnight. Do this each day, every day imagining some modicum of fulfillment for your self and make it a intention to look that success grow to be real. Now, exit there and accept as true with a greater you.

Bonus: Creating Other Positive Minds

Many oldsters which are true at some component, turn out to be training that detail later in lifestyles. One reason they do that is that coaching something to others lets you bear in mind that factor! I am now not asking that everyone who reads this ebook writes their non-public books, or opens their personal college of Positive Thinking, due to the truth that isn't always the characteristic of absolutely everyone in existence. This bankruptcy is ready the small daily possibilities that everyone should educate others and to unfold a touch little little little bit of happiness. Here you could find out some equipment with which you can unfold some of what you have got determined proper right here and at least upload a touch brightness to someone's day.

Think about how real it feels if a stranger smiles at you or if the character on the grocery checkout counter is happy for no purpose the least bit. The individuals who spread this form of small, random happiness are not surely supporting others, they may be additionally making themselves happier! Try smiling right now. You possibly felt handiest a hint bit happier right away. Maybe it became subtle, however it changed into there. Try it all over again :)

Human beings have a few issue known as "reflect neurons", it approach that we mirror the emotions of humans round us with out even searching for to. It way at the same time as a person offers us a actual smile on the road, we sense like smiling too. This is even real of a person we see on a tv, or in a photo. This little reality of lifestyles may be used as a exercise, with the aim of making positivity in extraordinary peoples' minds!

In a few techniques, the spreading of positivity could be an automatic problem. As you become someone with a extra first-rate thoughts, you will display greater positivity to the arena with out even trying. This is a first-rate trouble impact of a pleasant thoughts and if you choose out to feature positivity on your moves on a ordinary basis, the effect is probably surely good sized! As a long way as we are able to tell, there isn't a confined quantity of positivity inside the international. It isn't like you could get more with the aid of manner of manner of taking from others, in reality it is the alternative. The extra positivity that you show, the extra everybody round you'll have. And as human beings take a look at your example, they'll display the same positivity yet again to you. It is like you and every person round you are mirrors, reflecting positivity to and fro. Remember that "reflect neurons" do that with out us even attempting, so upload a similarly smile or a few kind phrases on your moves and observe what takes region. It might not be on the spot, but it'll at the least make you only a little bit happier proper away.

There is every exclusive problem to this small form of training that it's far proper to don't forget. People observe from and emulate those spherical them who set proper examples. As you exercise and increase a extra exceptional mind, you will set an example of a balanced, happier individual that others will want to emulate. Do not attempt to force this, it'll best get up sincerely over the years. But if someone asks you approximately some issue associated with what you found out through this method, then you definately definately definately are being furnished with a second in which to share a few thing of charge. Maybe you could tell them about a way to invite the query, to make and repeat a simple aim, or tell them approximately visualizing a exquisite thoughts. If they may be concerned though, perhaps you could tell them approximately this ebook if it feels proper. Again, the ones moments can handiest display up definitely out of their private hobby and questions. This e book isn't approximately knocking on human beings's doorways and spreading the phrase. The wonderful way to educate is to be the factor you preference to teach. A math trainer want to recognize math, and a song teacher need to understand track, so that you can handiest display others the way to have a exceptional mind whilst you're actually growing truely one of your very personal.

This final financial disaster is surely a few component to hold in the again of your mind as you exercising and increase over the years. Let the opportunities to unfold positivity come to you. If you keep your eyes open and feature a beginner's mind there can be lots of them! Life is complete of surprises, u.S.A.And downs, and the whole thing in among. The key to achievement is shifting and changing and the use of each opportunity to investigate and increase. If you are taking the number one steps, then you definitely definitely are already at the way. Welcome for your adventure within the path of a happier, greater healthy, and extra balanced existence. Everything that you need is already inner you. Just maintain in thoughts to use the ones easy device as lots as you could. Happy travels and happy minds!

## Chapter 26: What it Takes to Become a Positive Thinker

Anyone can become an constructive man or woman as long as one proactively makes the choice to pick first-class questioning. That is the splendor of being a person: you constantly have the freedom of choice. While it's far true that you can't constantly pick out to alternate your situation in life, you could however constantly choose out your mind about them. Notice what happens in the following state of affairs:

It is your birthday, and a cherished one determined to provide you a present. Upon seeing the wrapped discipline, you cannot help but bet as to what consists of indoors. An picture of something that you had been looking at the mall right away pops into your thoughts; you actually can't help but desire that it's far what is within the field.

You excitedly tear off the wrapping paper and what does it show? You can not assist thinking that it need to be the ugliest vase which you have ever seen. You proper away experience disappointed, but you try to conceal it due to the fact you do no longer need to harm the giver's emotions. Now, there are such a whole lot of opportunities as to what the subsequent step is probably for you.

If you have were given been a excellent character, however has an inclination to stay at the terrible, you may probably thank the giver and at the least try to fake to just like the present, but secretly stay on mind together with how ugly the vase is and on the way to get rid of it as speedy as each person is going domestic.

On the opportunity hand, if you were a brilliant truth seeker, you'll proper away word one correct exceptional of that vase (together with its color or form) and reputation on it. By doing so, you may in reality be appreciative of it and be capable of simply tell the giver that you love the coloration of this vase. Your excellent thoughts would possibly then preserve in mind the amazing manner to utilize the vase, now not due to the fact you need to satisfaction the giver, however because of the fact you understand the best features of that vase.

Based on this little scenario, you can see that first rate thinking is all approximately being selective with in which you consciousness your hobby. By deciding on to pay attention to the best, you'll be extra calm, satisfied, and content material material. It does not propose you are being unaware of faults of others; it simply way which you are aware about the negativity, however you choose out out to make the awesome out of the state of affairs.

People commonly base their mind on their emotions. Some genuinely have the addiction of right now appearing upon them. The fight or flight response is a clean instance of this. For example, at the same time as you notice a lion fame right within the the front of you, terror explodes to your thoughts and compels you to pick out amongst preventing back or run away as rapid as your legs can carry you. Your instinct to stay to tell the story is going on hyper-pressure and floods your body with adrenaline, permitting you to take without delay motion.

However, the contemporary international does no longer always call for one to at once translate feelings into motion all the time. The humans' combat or flight response has now advanced to allow one to address cutting-edge conditions, consisting of going through an angry boss, a dishonest partner, or an empty monetary organization account. There are an extended manner extra conditions now that permit one to take a step decrease back and count on in advance than taking motion. Negative feelings are despite the fact that your body's herbal manner of telling you that some factor is not right. But even as they will be experienced chronically, it'd bring about greater disastrous results, together with stress, tension, and despair. It is because of this that human beings, especially psychologists, pay plenty hobby to horrific emotions and a way to deal with them. It is due to this that brilliant emotions take a backseat in maximum human beings's minds. Positive emotions do no longer appear to be at once associated with any form of motion to maintain one's lifestyles from doom, this is why it is straightforward to take them as a right.

## Appreciate Positive Emotions

Barbara Fredrickson, a psychology professor, highlighted the importance of taking note of first-rate feelings, and this has led her to conceptualize the Broaden-and-Build Theory. This concept describes why effective emotions are important and why you want to admire them:

• They decorate your interest and thinking competencies. In precise phrases, you are probable to be more contemporary and open-minded whilst you're experiencing them.

• They relieve you from terrible emotions. For instance, continual stress is alleviated through manner of way of instilling contentment and satisfaction.

• They beautify your capacity to treatment problems and address tough situations. Positive emotions maintain you from falling into melancholy by means of way of letting you discover delight and comfort with others and internal yourself.

- They enhance your social, intellectual, physical, and mental nicely-being. For instance, effective emotions from spending amusing times with friends boosts your interpersonal skills, endorphins from exercising inspire you to enhance your bodily prowess, and the experience of satisfaction after reading a few component new boosts your choice to increase your statistics.

Positive feelings, normal with the idea, motive a higher life due to the truth they sell your preferred more healthful development.

## Chapter 27: 22 Tips on Positive Thinking

Manage Your Negative Emotions

To control your horrible feelings, you have to extend your Emotional Intelligence or EQ. To growth this, you may do the following: whenever you revel in a sure emotion, be it powerful or terrible, step one is to recognize the number one purpose that added on this emotion. Next, keep in mind the beliefs that motive you to experience the manner you do. After that, you may price on a scale of one to 10 the depth of that emotion. Finally, ask yourself whether the emotion is surely worth of a while and electricity. Once you have were given taken those steps, you may then hold in thoughts the excellent path of movement to cope with it.

For instance, permit's keep in mind a chum ignores your messages and it is making you revel in traumatic. Before growing with all kinds of guesses as to why your buddy isn't always replying, do your extraordinary to look at the emotion first. Is it certainly because of your pal's now not replying to you, or is there a greater extreme underlying trouble? Does the emotion cause bodily pain (collectively with a quick coronary heart rate and sweaty fingers)? How immoderate is it? Is the state of affairs in reality well well worth worrying over? By annoying about it, will you be capable of give you a solution? If no longer, what ought to be the right answer?

Here are some pointers on a way to remodel your terrible emotions into motion in a brilliant manner:

•	Expend all of that strength. If you're indignant or traumatic, take a stroll, pass on foot, swim, or any other wholesome form of exercise.

•	Talk it out. Face yourself in the replicate and speak it over. Let your thoughts flow out inside the form of terms most effective you could concentrate. Let it all out in private till you exhaust yourself. Then, flow into immediately to finding a logical answer.

•	Relax. If you experience beaten, take a breather by way of way of manner of paying attention to some fun music or taking a quick nap. You do no longer need to be on this type of rush all the time.

- Socialize. Talk to a chum or on your pup approximately the problem. Let the wild emotion fade away with the useful resource of attractive with others for a while.

- Do a few aspect nice. If you want window buying, then go to the mall and test some matters. If you want painting or writing poems, translate the emotion thru your artwork. If you are out of mind, choose out up a mop or a broom and clean your home; doing all your chores is in reality a cheap form of remedy.

Beware, despite the fact that, of vain techniques of dealing with horrible emotions. While they may appear powerful, they truly cause a downward spiral that can motive even worse situations and feelings inside the destiny. The most not unusual of these are: turning to pills and alcohol, intentionally avoiding the trouble, doing passive topics together with oversleeping and searching an excessive amount of tv, and heading off socialization.

Retrain Your Brain

The mind is a powerful organ, controlling all of the frame's important capabilities, which include all human feelings. The thoughts has such control over the frame that highbrow pressure, consisting of being burdened or feeling pressured, can cause bodily responses in the frame, which incorporates nausea, headaches, and dizziness. But another terrific element of the brain is its capability to examine, exchange, and adapt. This technique you may alternate how you suspect and the manner you respond to topics round you. You can circumstance your brain to grow to be more tremendous.

The human mind keeps to have a study and increase, and exquisite parts of the brain which can be exercised greater, inclusive of those answerable for reminiscence, or cognition, increase huge, that is why even older people can nevertheless examine new talents, or cope with new art work that is very high-quality from what that they had finished in the past. In the identical revel in, you can educate yourself new methods of reacting or responding to horrible activities. Such as in cases of disappointment, in preference to preserving immediately to the remorse for a long time, or even throwing blame in the direction of others, you can consciously choose to permit pass of those regrets, and as you continue to hone this new mindset, it becomes much less tough until it's far almost second nature. In truth, through being greater positive and powerful, the thoughts can treatment troubles quicker and extra efficiently, in comparison to times whilst the mind is flooded with horrible emotions and pessimism in the path of the viable results.

Calm the Mind

In order on the way to have excellent thoughts, you want to start at the impartial quarter, with being at peace and conscious, without being judgmental of who you are, what you do, and some thing happens round you. Before panicking, annoying, or falling into melancholy, take a 2nd to reflect: is it really so hopeless? Is there without a doubt nothing you could do? Is it definitely that huge a deal? Once you ask your self the ones questions calmly, you could moreover solution them gently. By now, you may have a choice, to be a pessimist or an optimist, and aware choice may be very essential within the choice to be a exceptional truth seeker.

One of the commonplace methods to find peace or calmness is conscious meditation, it absolutely is an offshoot of conventional Buddhist meditation. Here, you may make the effort away, find out a quiet, snug spot, and reflect upon your modern mind and movements without being vital of them. In this workout, you want to awareness exceptional on the winning, paying no interest to beyond regrets or fears regarding the destiny. See handiest what is going on, only those topics which can be inside the right right here and now, and you may experience your issues and issues soften away, you may be capable of revel in and appreciate your life without it being muddled through trivial worries. You may be able to discover the center of your being that defines you and what your happiness want to be, no longer subjected to outside difficulties or fears. This will alleviate your stress and deliver manner to a healthy and powerful kingdom of mind. Along with this, there are bodily advantages as well, together with more potent immunity and better sleep styles.

Focus on the Good Things

How happy you're with the way you also are affects the manner you respond to the arena. People frequently have the tendency to be over essential of themselves and often popularity on what they expect they do not have or do now not have enough of. This tendency motives terrible thoughts to flood the mind, making you greater stressed and disheartened. This is why it is so important to attention at the powerful subjects in a unmarried's life in preference to the terrible, the lacking, or the missing.

When you replicate upon your existence, your activity, or perhaps your appearance, commonly remind your self of the great things first and be satisfied with what you find. Accept that that is how it's miles and apprehend what you have got got. Things simplest seem the manner they're in step with the way you pick to see them, there are many aspects in lifestyles you can not manipulate, specifically the subjects which are out of doors to you, however what you have entire control over is the way you choose to look subjects and what you choose to preserve to the foreground. For instance, at the same time as getting a switch at art work, you can choose out out to assume that your artwork end up unsatisfactory on your manager, or which you are not critical to the organization, but you could moreover select to look it as a mission because of the truth your better americaaccept as real with you may deal with a contemporary hobby, or as an opportunity if you want to hone greater capabilities and higher your self. You can be worrying and doubt your self over the preceding, or you could come to paintings with eagerness and optimism on the ultra-modern opportunities due to the latter.

Use the Power of Affirmations

As is already hooked up, the mind is a powerful element, however once in a while, you may discover your self wondering in a way which you deem unstable. This is in which affirmations are available in. Affirmations may be a way a great way to talk with yourself deeply and concretely, so one can recognize what it is you really need in existence, and what's sincerely critical to you. There are some posted booklets of affirmations that you can use that target a sure concern consider, which includes getting over heartbreak or to be encouraged, however you can additionally write your non-public affirmations consistent with what you need to acquire.

When writing your own affirmations, make sure to stay outstanding, within the gift, targeted, and deeply personal, this is approximately you notwithstanding the whole lot. Try to attention on a nice goal, along facet turning into more affected person with others if you have a mood, then you could make affirmations that will help you together with your aim, however moreover remember to hold it conceivable to your unconscious. Instead of "I will never lose my mood" you can say, "I is probably extra forgiving and calm in a tough situation" and deliver yourself the risk to broaden.

Affirmations are smooth and useful gear in changing the manner you act and feel, allowing you to grow to be the kind of man or woman you need to be.

Keep a Positive Body Image

Society's necessities of beauty may be high, nearly no longer viable, for each men and women. People are bombarded with photos of the 'nice body' or the 'ideal face', and feelings of inadequacy or even of being undesirable can eat every body.

By no method are you defined with the aid of way of your look. You are lots extra than your body type, length, or seems, and that could be a few factor you need to understand. However, the way you understand your frame can trade the way you apprehend your internal self. If you're vital of your frame, or think you're unattractive, you can think you aren't in reality well worth of love, understand, and appreciation, even from your self. But in case you discover ways to see your frame with generosity and love, so shall you look upon your internal self with generosity and love. Your concept of self esteem is not outside to you, how others see you is secondary to the manner you notice your self.

Start through specializing in super topics about your frame in place of the terrible subjects. Instead of obsessing over wrinkles and blemishes, study the additives of your frame which you are happy with, like how your hair falls over your face, or how your lashes are mainly prolonged. If you discover this tough, absolutely hold in mind how complicated and wonderful the human body is, how tens of millions of cells are going for walks to hold you alive and healthy, how every muscle and bone are coordinated simply so you can dance or run. You will in no way run out of things to apprehend about your body.

Exercise

Regular exercising will maintain our our bodies in tip-top form, and will also advantage our minds. Being active is an essential a part of being a effective fact seeker, being alert and organized to achieve this technique a can-do thoughts-set that is worthwhile if you want to obtain achievement. Exercise can cause you to have higher mood patterns, be extra active and save you many common ailments because of the sedentary life-style maximum human beings have nowadays. Exercise is thought to bolster the release of endorphins that can also heighten emotions of happiness.

Before beginning on an exercising habitual however, make certain to be aware about your frame's abilties and obstacles. Overexerting your self on the primary day may also discourage you from following it up; try and do it slowly and absolutely. It is likewise practical to dispel any unreasonable expectancies from workout. You may not be able to run a 1/2-mile in your first strive at strolling, nor will you get abs after in step with week of sit down down-ups, try now not to reputation on the way you want to glance through exercising, but greater on how a wonderful deal extra healthy you may be, how your thoughts will benefit, and what form of happier exercising your body can make you.

Eat Healthy

Loving your frame equals giving it the vitamins it wishes and staying a ways from any food which could have destructive effects in your health. Fast meals and junk food can also flavor appropriate, but those are fairly lousy and may purpose fast weight gain, particularly if coupled with little to no workout, foremost to obesity, diabetes, and coronary heart troubles.

As a rule of thumb, consider to devour more leafy vegetables, end result, complete grains, and fish to your clean meals. Cut decrease back or surely commonly keep away from candies, processed, baked gadgets, and fried rapid food similarly to sensitive sugars collectively with carbonated gentle beverages, goodies, and sugary breads.

Along with actual nutrients, wholesome consuming conduct are also a want to. Eat efficaciously, do not gorge yourself and do now not starve your self. Eating too little can gradual down your metabolism or maybe reason faster weight benefit. Try to stop ingesting at the same time as you begin feeling entire, do no longer wait till you're crammed, lessening your each day calorie consumption.

Remember, you could manipulate your weight clearly by way of ingesting healthy and some light exercising. But do now not be discouraged even as you do no longer get the results you desired, do it for the sake of your fitness and outlook, not for a dress duration.

## Chapter 28: Have Adequate Sleep

The adequacy of your sleep is sincerely as vital as how active you are. Having terrible sleep can affect the ranges of stress hormones, immunity, or maybe heighten risks for coronary heart sickness, not to say it could simply have an impact on our mood as nicely. You have a propensity to be after a harassed, sleep deprived night.

To have proper enough sleep, it's miles vital to recognize how lots sleep you need and characteristic regular sleeping styles. If you are sleepy after dozing 7 hours, try to go to bed half-hour earlier subsequent time and so forth, until you discover the most beneficial length of sleep you want, at the equal time as you wake feeling the maximum rested. Also, try to visit bed on the equal time every night and regularize your slumbering and waking times. This will set your inner clock and let you have plenty less problem even as in search of to sleep.

Focus On The Present!

Worrying over the last or agonizing over the future is laborious and lets in nobody. Having hobby is essential to being happy. Without focus, our mind has a tendency to wander, and additional regularly than not, it wanders toward bad subjects in region of the remarkable things. Isn't it real which you frequently bear in mind the rent extra even as you think you is probably quick for the month than if you have paid your hire on time?

Being centered within the present allows you to view it in a realistic way and lets in you as a way to make aware selections on the manner you need to revel in approximately matters. You can CHOOSE to recognize the exquisite things within the now instead of what dissatisfies you. When you seize yourself wondering negatively closer to your self or others, try and take it lower back with a compliment, or recognition on a nice difficulty. Focus at the triumphing allows you to take nicely timed movement and keeps you away from useless worry. Studies have proven that folks who are focused on their obligations have a propensity to be happier human beings in vicinity of folks who regularly have their minds wander off. Is it recognition that makes human beings happier, or are unhappy human beings simply greater prone to be out of region in concept due to the fact they discover the present dull or unsatisfactory? Either way, improving your recognition can lead you to be extra green, and thereby, greater satisfied, with yourself and make you extra green, alert and energetic in pursuing your desires.

Find Substantial, Simple Pleasures

Although happiness is a more long time concept than satisfaction, you can derive extended-term happiness through finding clean pleasures in the midst of the every day grind. It is a false impression that finding pleasure in little subjects is a childish best. It is vital to derive pleasure from little topics in order that our happiness does not depend upon one key trouble that, if it is going awry, can disrupt the complete, which encompass first-rate focusing on paintings, one's look, or one's reputation.

You can find pleasure in a grin from someone cherished, the maintain in thoughts of a near buddy, or perhaps a cloud fashioned like an elephant. If you discover ways to apprehend those clean pleasures, you can make happiness enlarge and enhance it every day. Remember that happiness is a country of being you choose to be in, not the dollars in a financial enterprise account or a huge advertising at the save you of the day. What exact do these types of do if you do no longer enjoy your every day existence?

There also are people who do not forget that allowing your self pleasures can purpose you to be an awful lot much less effective, and pride can be purpose for someone to get away the fact they discover insupportable, however clean, healthful pleasures can maintain you satisfied and in fact make you greater effective. This is the cause that most work locations invest loads of coins in gyms, holidays, and a laugh outings. Have Meaning in Your Life

A purposeless existence is an empty life, and a frivolous lifestyles is a superficial life, like a residence of gambling cards positive to disintegrate in the long run. It is crucial to find fulfillment and which means that in a few difficulty it's miles you do. Great fulfillment may be derived from the unquenchable preference to broaden, mature, and enhance even as people are doing topics they may be captivated with. You can find success in some thing you do now not truely contend with, but is not success in a location you love plenty extra a laugh? And if you so love a fantastic discipline, in any other case you take delivery of as proper with that what you do subjects, aren't you even extra driven to be successful?

Leading a extraordinary existence with tough paintings and distinct characteristic might not be amusing and clean, but expertise you have got integrity and that you are doing a little component profitable will give you a enjoy of well being and may lead you to finding real happiness and contentment. Doing something great for you and pursuing it with electricity will help you find out your actual functionality, as opposed to doing obligations which you do not in reality cope with mechanically. Pursuing which means that for your lifestyles will will will let you develop as someone, make you surer of yourself, bolster self-self warranty, and give you a experience of fulfillment that ultimately leads to long-time period happiness.

Realize Self-Determination

The precept of self-determination keeps that with a purpose to be satisfied and triggered, there are three, clean well-known desires that human beings ought to understand; mainly, autonomy, competency, and relatedness. These three desires need to be fostered and supported in order with a view to acquire utmost productivity, creativity, and functioning. On the opportunity hand, if the ones desires are overlooked or curtailed, there are also terrible consequences for your properly-being.

Autonomy is all people's want to determine their life, their course, their art work, or their loves. In a enjoy, it method freedom, that is a important a part of anybody's existence. If you have got were given the capacity to determine what it's miles you want to do in your existence, you may revel in extra endorsed to conducting your dreams, which could in all likelihood cause greater achievement, and statistics that you are unfastened to stay the existence you want lets in you to manual a happier life.

Competence is a person's need to sense in a characteristic and confident in something it's far they do. Getting an encouraging praise or commendation for a manner properly accomplished will make a person revel in more delivered on in doing their method, even increasing productivity and commonplace health. On the opportunity hand, feeling inept in a first-rate mission can discourage creativity and growth.

Relatedness is the need for someone to make deep and real connections to others round them. Having meaningful, but autonomic and in a position relationships is a crucial want for all of us to be actually glad.

Hone Your Talents and Develop Your Skills

The belief that so that you can excel in a positive area calls for 'genius' is a false impression that would curtail your choice to expand new competencies and sharpen abilities you may already own. It is also unaware of the fact that the folks who excel at their craft had been no longer born to excellence, they likely worked very difficult at it, devoting their time and electricity in turning into the masters that they have turn out to be.

The men and women who're professionals or masters in their craft have earned the select out thru blood, sweat and tears, and because of this you will be an professional in some element too, if you consciously decide to increase your talents or hone your talents. But always bear in mind that this will take tough art work, subject and the right motivations to your detail. Pursuing and devoting your self to analyzing or developing a knowledge or skills is its personal closing reward. Free yourself from the notion that pleasant innately talented humans can expect to achieve success. No one is born an professional, even Mozart, considered a genius at a young age, have emerge as as top as he modified into because of the truth he pursued his love of music and acquired schooling as a baby. So if you are obsessed on some thing, do it, hold doing it, and artwork hard.

Strengthen and Develop Your Character

Your individual is a reflected photo of your morals, and what you remember well and horrible conduct. Morality additionally units your motivations, whether or not or no longer you're doing some detail for the incorrect or proper reasons. Basically, it way doing the proper thing, although it's miles more hard or maybe volatile, sincerely because of the fact it is right.

www.ingramcontent.com/pod-product-compliance
Lightning Source LLC
Chambersburg PA
CBHW050408120526
44590CB00015B/1877